TEENS ~ SOCIAL SKILL STRATEGIES

Facilitator Reproducible Activities for Groups and Individuals

Ester R.A. Leutenberg
Carol Butler, MS Ed, RN, C

Illustrated by
Amy L. Brodsky, LISW-S

Duluth, Minnesota

Whole Person
101 West 2nd St., Suite 203
Duluth, MN 55802

800-247-6789

books@wholeperson.com
www.wholeperson.com

Teens – Social Skill Strategies
Facilitator Reproducible Activities for Groups and Individuals

Printed in the United States of America

10 9 8 7 6 5 4 3 2 1

Editorial Director: Carlene Sippola
Art Director: Joy Morgan Dey

Library of Congress Control Number: 2013954258
ISBN: 978-157025-306-5

Purpose of the Book

Action and reflection promote learning.

In this workbook, *TEENS – Social Skill Strategies,* teens learn by doing, from each other, and through thought and feedback.

Real life comes to the classroom, group room or individual space as teens practice new skills or begin to change negative behaviors. Awareness of societal expectations, empathy, ethics and altruism are not taught but are lived, through simulated and actual situations.

Social skills constitute more than a time-honored list of modern manners; they are ways to thrive in today's world. Whether texting or talking, sitting at the table or involved in a crisis situation, operating with family or friends, in school or in love, communication, courtesy and compassion triumph.

Verbal and non-verbal communication, social graces, the desire to fit in, diversity, inclusion, finding and being a friend, family relationships, forgiveness, first love, breakups, humanitarianism and other topics are featured. Social issues, including abuse prevention and other topics are addressed.

Experiential education occurs as teens practice ways to achieve these goals.

- Become a leader
- Be a team player
- Portray and interpret body language
- Launch and join a conversation
- Use, not abuse, technological communication
- Elicit and express opinions
- Enact and analyze social behavior
- Read and write poetry, songs, lyrics, letters and riddles, expressing feelings related to relationships
- Develop passion for and ways to promote a social cause
- Start or participate in a service club

Active learning occurs as teens consider social life and social consciousness through interactive games, introspective drawing and writing, mock videos, role plays, panel discussions, press conferences, through drama, music, pantomimes and other activities.

Teens will practice ways to build people up and break down barriers.

Teens will internalize Maya Angelou's message:

***I've learned that people will forget what you said,
people will forget what you did,
but people will never forget how you made them feel.***

Format of the Book

An Introduction for Teen Participants motivates teens for the activities (Page vi).

A Cover Page for each chapter provides a quotation and description of the sessions. This page may be distributed as an introduction to a workshop or series of sessions.

Seven Chapters, four to ten sessions per chapter, (total of forty-seven) encompass the following:

1. **Communication**
   Body language, personal space, behavioral cues, active listening, conversations, first impressions, communication starters and stoppers, assertiveness and negotiation skills.
2. **Expectations**
   Technology, social networking, mealtime, introductions, first dates, events, travel, condolences, diplomacy, job interviews, work relationships and sportsmanship.
3. **Fitting In**
   Parent/caregiver issues, excessive people pleasing, acceptance of self and others, respectful disagreement, shyness, positive personality traits, newcomers, diversity and multicultural contributions to society.
4. **Friendship**
   Positive peer support, non-aggression, frenemies, influence of words and actions, friendship lyrics, envy and jealousy, and helping a person in crisis.
5. **Family**
   Traditional and non-traditional family styles, changes at home, sibling rivalry, respect for authority without fear or rebellion, and forgiveness.
6. **Teen Love**
   Healthy and unhealthy relationships, parent/caregiver concerns, first love, expression through art and poetry, dating dilemmas, breakups and power principles.
7. **Caring**
   Empathy, social causes, creative fundraisers, ways to help at home, school, community, etc., advocacy in action, leadership as a passion to serve versus self-serving power.

Each chapter may function as a workshop. Provide one session per day or week. Promote themes through posters and flyers. Emphasize the interactive and collaborative nature of the sessions.

Each of the forty-seven sessions may stand alone. Pick and choose per your population.

Most sessions are adaptable to interactive or individual activities. Most require at least fifty minutes and if necessary can be continued the next session or for homework.

In Each Session

Reproducible handout(s) for participants (games, charades, questions, etc.) Read before session, cut on the broken lines if directed, white out or add text specific to your teens if necessary, and photocopy.

A *For the Facilitator* page on the back of each teen handout provides the following:

I. Purpose: Goals for teens.
II. General Comments: Brief background information.
III. Possible Activities: Ideas to introduce and present topics. Answer keys or responses to elicit.
IV. Enrichment Activities: Additional learning opportunities. Ways to close session or follow up.

Sensitive subjects are addressed. Facilitator discretion is advised. Teens need to be reminded that the supreme social skill is to seek help for oneself or a peer in trouble. Facilitators need to refer teens in crisis for a psychiatric evaluation or to emergency services.

Suggestions for Facilitating

Capitalize on the likelihood that peers are of primary importance to teens.
Consider the classroom, group room and/or individual space as a learning lab where teens experiment with behaviors.
Expect movement, discussion, laughter and learning from each other.

Teens – Social Skill Strategies sessions simulate life and provide practice for situations that may be unfamiliar and uncomfortable. Teens who are shy in real life may be reluctant to role play; teens who tend toward prejudice may question the value of diversity. The activities are arranged to motivate change.

As a facilitator, your skills will help teens gently move outside their comfort zones.
Emphasize that teens may volunteer to participate (or not).
Encourage teens to gradually test the waters.
(*Example*: write, draw, share, be a team member and/or eventually become a leader.)
Suggest that the higher the level of participation, the greater the benefits.
Promote the value of taking risks in session, risks that they wouldn't take in real life.
(*Example*: Start or join an ongoing conversation during a role play.)
Persuade teens to *Just do it* – but be mindful of your responsibility to others.
(*Example*: let lyrics flow without worrying whether they're wonderful).
Location matters. Expect team members to sit together, arrange chairs in clusters as needed, for some activities a circle is a friendlier forum than rows; for mock videos or role plays, set up a stage area and audience seating.
For activities that involve social causes, fundraising, leadership, etc., try to promote actual charitable connections and actions; maybe teens can start a service club if feasible in your facility.
Decide the level of interaction or introspection your teens need and can handle; although most sessions promote peer contact, many activities can be done as individual worksheets.
Make the setting safe; ask teens to brainstorm their own ground rules.

Possibilities:

- Use name codes (example – for a friend who likes to boss, use LTB - Likes To Boss).
- Respect people who are reluctant to share.
- Keep private what people say in class or group. *"What's said in this room, stays in this room."*
- Game contestants may ask team members for help as needed.
- There are few right or wrong answers; on paper or in games, state what is true for you.
- Open your mind to consider other views, cultures, lifestyles, etc.
- No put-downs when ideas differ.
- No mocking if someone's behaviors seem awkward.
- Encourage peers to join in activities (as you will learn to include people in real life).
- Listen actively without interrupting the speaker.
- If you or a peer feel like harming self or others, tell a trusted adult.

Remind teens that the group is a segment of society – skills acquired here transfer to the outside.

Our gratitude to the following for their input ~
Annette Damien, MS, PPS and Hanna Lavoie, teenager
And to these professionals who make us look good!
Art Director – Joy Dey
Editor and Lifelong Teacher – Eileen Regen
Editorial Director – Carlene Sippola
Illustrator – Amy L. Brodsky
Proofreader – Jay Leutenberg

Introduction for Teen Participants

Social networking, friends, family, dating and love – what could be more important?
How do you deal with your own and others' sensitive situations?
How do you handle your own and others' differences?
On a wider scale, what do you care about?

In ***Teens – Social Skill Strategies*** you and your peers are partners in learning.

You will expand your social comfort zone as you work on many skills:

1) Mix, mingle, observe and give feedback to each other.
2) Pick up on and portray body language cues.
3) Practice ways to make a good first impression.
4) Become a better conversationalist (on dates, with friends and your own family, with your friends' or a partner's family, new people, co-workers, teachers, etc.).
5) Assert your opinions and settle conflicts.
6) Figure out *fitting in* – without bending over backwards, with positive personality traits, overcoming shyness, and by welcoming new and different people and ideas.
7) Find friends not *frenemies*. Operate without envy and jealousy.
8) Manage family issues and handle authority figures people at home and elsewhere.
9) Forgive others and yourself, and learn to apologize.
10) Express feelings about romantic love; understand power in relationships and heal from breakups.
11) Develop leadership skills and possibly create a club or organization.

Social skill strategy activities are fun!

- Team Activities
- Charades and picture games
- Game shows
- Talk shows
- Tic-Tac-Toe
- Bingo
- Role plays
- Mock videos
- Pantomime and freeze frames
- Match games
- Panels and press conferences
- Poetry, songs and lyrics
- Riddles
- Art

Additionally, you will have other opportunities to think for yourself, share if you wish, and interact.

Major Social Skill

I've learned that people will forget what you said,
people will forget what you did,
but people will never forget how you made them feel.

– Maya Angelou

Teens – *Social Skill Strategies*

TABLE OF CONTENTS

COMMUNICATION 1

You never know when a moment and a few sincere words can have an impact on a life.

~ ZIG ZIGLAR

Body Language "Says" It All

1. tight-lipped	2. pout with bottom lip out	3. bite lip	4. roll eyes	5. fake smile
6. hand over mouth	7. tilt head to the side	8. head down	9. chin up	10. cross arms in front of chest
11. raise eyebrows, tilt head	12. arms clasped behind head	13. thumbs down	14. hand on heart	15. shifty eyes
16. fingers up, hands facing outward	17. stand, legs a couple feet apart, hands on hips	18. index finger and thumb touch, other fingers up	19. thumbs up	20. pull on ear
21. shrug shoulders	22. hands over ears	23. tap foot	24. yawn	25. slumped over
26. look down	27. fidget with hair	28. glare with eyes	29. hands relaxed on the sides	30. body language doesn't match words

Body Language "Says" It All

FOR THE FACILITATOR

I. Purpose

To identify common non-verbal cues.

II. General Comments

Sensitivity to others' facial expressions and body language enhances one's ability to receive messages; awareness of non-verbal cues helps teens monitor impressions they convey.

III. Possible Activities

a. Before session photocopy the *Body Language "Says" it All* handout and cut on the broken lines.
b. Place the cutouts face down in a cup.
c. Before session, coach a volunteer to enter the room and grip his/her own arms.
d. Volunteer walks in with arms crossed, hands hugging upper arms.
e. Ask teens to pretend the room temperature is 55 degrees Fahrenheit.
f. Ask teens what is conveyed (person is cold).
g. Ask what the body language suggests if the room is 75 degrees Fahrenheit (resistant).
h. Explain the importance of context in deciphering body language, to look for clusters of behavior (more than one sign) and cultural factors. *Example:* someone who crosses their arms may be cold or they may be resistant, depending on the situation.
i. Teens alternately go to the front of the room, pick a cutout and portray the action(s).
j. Peers guess the messages conveyed and share times they experienced the feelings.
k. Examples of common meanings (cutout numbers correspond to the numbers below):

1. secretive	2. annoyed	3. tense
4. exasperated	5. dislike	6. shock
7. interested	8. embarrassment	9. pride
10. resistant	11. questioning	12. confident
13. disapproval	14. attempt to show truthfulness	15. untrustworthy
16. a signal to stop	17. authoritative	18. *okay* (in some cultures it is a vulgar sign)
19. approval	20. unsure	21. does not care
22. doesn't want to hear what's being said	23. impatient	24. disinterest
25. defeated	26. lack of self-confidence	27. anxious
28. anger	29. open to talk	30. doesn't mean what person is saying

IV. Enrichment Activity

Encourage teens to share times theirs' or others' face and body language revealed true feelings.

Congruent Conversation

You can say one thing but show another with your facial expression and body language.

Example:
Your acquaintance asks you to help him move on Saturday.
You say *Yes* and roll your eyes.

In the situations below place an **S** if the words and actions send the **same** message and a **D** if **different**.

1. ______ Dating partner says *You're the only one I want* and then whistles at a passerby.
2. ______ Teen says Y*es, I'll clean the garage* and then slams down a backpack.
3. ______ Teen promises *won't text and drive* and then puts cell phone in trunk.
4. ______ Friend says *Tell me all about it* and then reads a text message.
5. ______ Teen says *Let me help you* and then carries a person's package.

When you are genuine, your actions won't give you away and will be congruent with your words. Below are examples of ways to diplomatically speak the truth that correspond to the *different* messages above:

1. Dating partner says *I'd like us to date other people.*
2. Teen says *I'd rather clean the garage on the week-end when I'm not tired from school.*
4. Friend says *I'd like to hear about it in fifteen minutes after I've checked my messages.*

By drawing pictures, cartoons, caricatures, or using symbols, speech balloons or thought bubbles, depict and/or describe a situation where your mouth said one thing and your body revealed another.

Substitute truthful but tactful words for the above mixed message:

____

____

Congruent Conversation

FOR THE FACILITATOR

I. Purpose

To recognize incongruence between words and facial expression and/or body language.
To substitute truth and tact for mixed messages.

II. General Comments

People may *tell all* with eye rolls, fixed gazes on cell phone screens, yawns, foot taps, etc.

III. Possible Activities

a. Before session coach two volunteers to perform the following role play:
   - One asks *This week-end will you help me baby-sit my two-year-old triplet nephews?*
   - The other looks down and shakes head no then looks up and says *"Oh, sure."*

b. When session starts, volunteers perform the skit.

c. Ask the audience peers if the person really wanted to help babysit (no).

d. Ask how teens knew the person didn't want to help (shook head *no*).

e. Write *Congruent* and *Incongruent* on the board; ask their definitions (similar, different).

f. Explain that words and actions can be congruent or incongruent.

g. Distribute the *Congruent Conversation* handout; teens read the information aloud.

h. Direct teens to complete their drawings and/or descriptions of incongruent conversations.

i. Reinforce that artistic talent is not required and teens need not edit for grammar or spelling.

j. Encourage teens to share their pictures and/or descriptions. Remind them to use name codes.

k. Encourage teens to share their truthful but tactful word substitutions.

l. Ask teens to team up in pairs or trios and role play situations they have witnessed or experienced where words and actions did not match.

m. After each role play, actors and audience identify truthful but tactful responses that would have prevented the incongruent scenarios.

IV. Enrichment Activities

a. Ask teens to brainstorm times they might need to do something they dislike and monitor their actions instead of changing their words (for social grace or kindness).

   Possibilities

   - You're introduced to a person whose hand you don't want to shake, but the person extends his/her right hand; you shake the person's hand firmly.
   - A lonely neighbor starts a conversation when you'd rather talk on your cell phone; you ignore the phone and focus on the neighbor for a few minutes.
   - As you're told *Stick to the speed limit*, you want to grab the car keys and run; you listen patiently to the advice.
   - An elderly relative tells you a story you have heard three times and you want to roll your eyes; you make eye contact and listen.
   - A caregiver asks you to get some groceries but you'd rather watch music videos; you smile and say *Okay*.

SPACE INVADERS

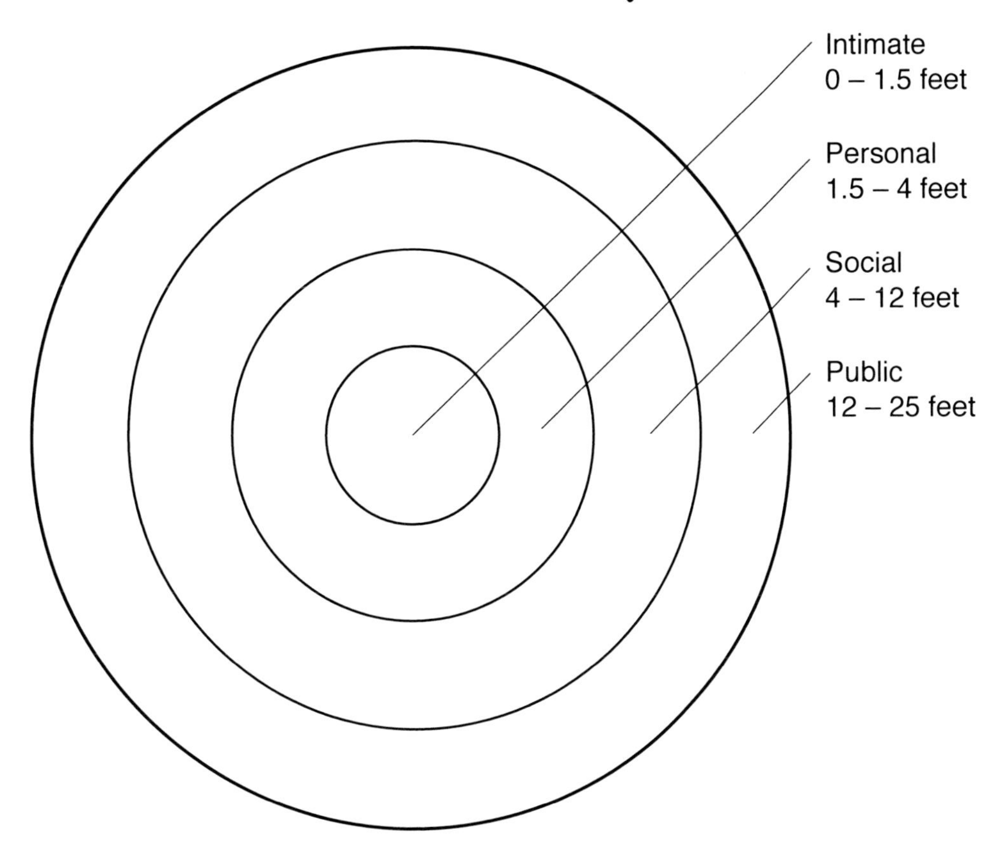

Write the correct spatial distance letter on the line in front of the relationship description.

A. Intimate B. Personal C. Social D. Public

1. ________ Acquaintances at a business meeting
2. ________ Speaker and audience
3. ________ Couples or partners
4. ________ Close friends and family

Describe a time someone invaded your intimate or personal space. ____________________

____

____

How did you feel? ____

____

____

In what ways can you respect others' space bubbles? ______________________________

____

____

SPACE INVADERS

FOR THE FACILITATOR

I. Purpose

To recognize and respect spatial distances for different relationships and occasions.
To maintain boundaries when necessary regarding one's intimate and personal space.

II. General Comments

Proxemics addresses spatial distances among people as they interact. Social skills are enhanced when teens behave according to society's expectations and people's comfort zones.

III. Possible Activities

a. Ask teens to divide into two lines, stand on opposite sides of the room or as far away as possible.
b. Teens opposite each other are partners; facilitator plays partner if an uneven number are present.
c. Ask teens to slowly walk toward their partners until one or both say STOP due to uncomfortable closeness.
d. Teens note the distance between partners (it may be around or more than four feet).
e. Ask partners to continue walking toward each other, arms at sides, until they are almost touching.
f. Ask teens to describe their comfort levels as space shrinks (they may feel anxious).
g. Teens resume their seats.
h. Explain that most people have invisible space bubbles around them; getting closer causes discomfort.
i. Distribute the *Space Invaders* handout and ask volunteers to read aloud the labels next to the circles.
j. Allow time for completion; Answer key: 1.C, 2.D, 3.A, 4.B.
k. Encourage teens to share answers.
l. Some ways to respect others' space bubbles: Keep the appropriate distance for the relationship or situation and if someone leans away, it is time to back off.
m. Encourage a discussion of ways to make their own space boundaries known.
Examples:
Ask people to step back or to not follow too closely; if someone tries to hug and you prefer not to be hugged, extend your hand for a handshake or a pat on the arm.

IV. Enrichment Activities

a. Ask for volunteers who will pantomime. Coach *actors* by giving them the instructions privately. After each performance, ask audience what infringement occurred and how the person whose space was invaded might feel and how they might handle the space invasions portrayed in the pantomimes.

SCENARIOS

- A teen is typing on a computer or cell phone. A peer gets very close and looks over the teen's shoulder.
- (Tell audience the setting is an elevator). Two or three teens face forward as if looking at the elevator door; a person enters, stands too close to someone and faces the person instead of the door.
- (Tell audience the setting involves strangers at a movie). Use two chairs as props. One crowds the other by putting an arm across the back of the chair.

b. Ask teens to create and pantomime other scenarios; discuss discomfort and feelings.

Communication Cues

When you observe body language and are sensitive to feelings, people share because they feel understood.

Example

You walk into your home and your sibling is pacing, head down.
Comment on what you see: *You look stressed.*

Your sibling says *I flunked my math test.*
Paraphrase (put in your own words what was said):
You're worried you'll fail the course.

Your sibling says *I'll lose my driving privileges if my grades go down.*
Reflect feelings: *You're afraid you'll lose what's really important to you.*

Your sibling says *My friends won't like having to take buses.*
Clarify what you think is meant: *Is your major concern how your friends might react?*

Your sibling says *Yes, that's the worst part, but it might also affect getting into a training program.*
Summarize the situation: *So, flunking the test could seriously hurt your social life and your career plans.*

Now it's your turn to practice.

What (suspected) emotion has someone at home shown? Write a comment you could have made.

Comment ______________________________

Put into your own words what the person might have said.

Paraphrase ______________________________

What might you have said to show you picked up on the person's feelings?

Reflect ______________________________

What might you have asked to be sure you understood the situation?

Clarify ______________________________

How might the person have answered your question? ______________________________

How might you have tied it all together to prove you understood?

Summarize ______________________________

Communication Cues

FOR THE FACILITATOR

I. Purpose

To develop observational and active listening skills.

II. General Comments

Teens have opportunity to perceive and ask about recognizing behavioral signals, paraphrasing, reflecting feelings, asking for clarification and summarizing.

III. Possible Activities

a. Before session coach a teen to walk into room, slam down book and put head on desk.
b. Discuss the word *observational.*
c. When session starts, the teen portrays the above actions.
d. Ask group what might be going on with the person (angry, sad, disappointed, etc.).
e. Ask how we can suspect a person's emotional state (observe behavioral cues).
f. Ask teens if assumptions are always right (no, we need more information from the person).
g. State that open ended questions (that elicit more than a brief *yes, no* or one word response) are excellent, but other techniques also encourage communication.
h. Distribute the *Communication Cues* handout and ask teens to read aloud the text above and in the box.
i. Allow time to complete the handout.
j. List on the board the communication cues:
   - Comment
   - Paraphrase
   - Reflect
   - Clarify
   - Summarize
k. Encourage teens to share their responses; write responses on the board as teens dictate.
l. Encourage peers to give feedback and other suggestions for each technique.
m. Encourage a discussion regarding the advantages of these techniques over open-ended questions.

   Possibilities
   - Questions can seem like interrogation by an authority figure even if asked by a peer.
   - Questions make some people defensive.
   - Most people will confirm or refute and elaborate on an observation about their emotions.
   - These techniques show the listener *gets it* or understands the situation and feelings.

IV. Enrichment Activities

a. Ask teens to role play situations they imagine or have experienced and use the techniques.
b. Encourage teens to portray positive situations first (like teens sharing that they were accepted into their chosen college or a discussion about a great first date).
c. Peers provide feedback.

Conversations

Launching Conversations with New People

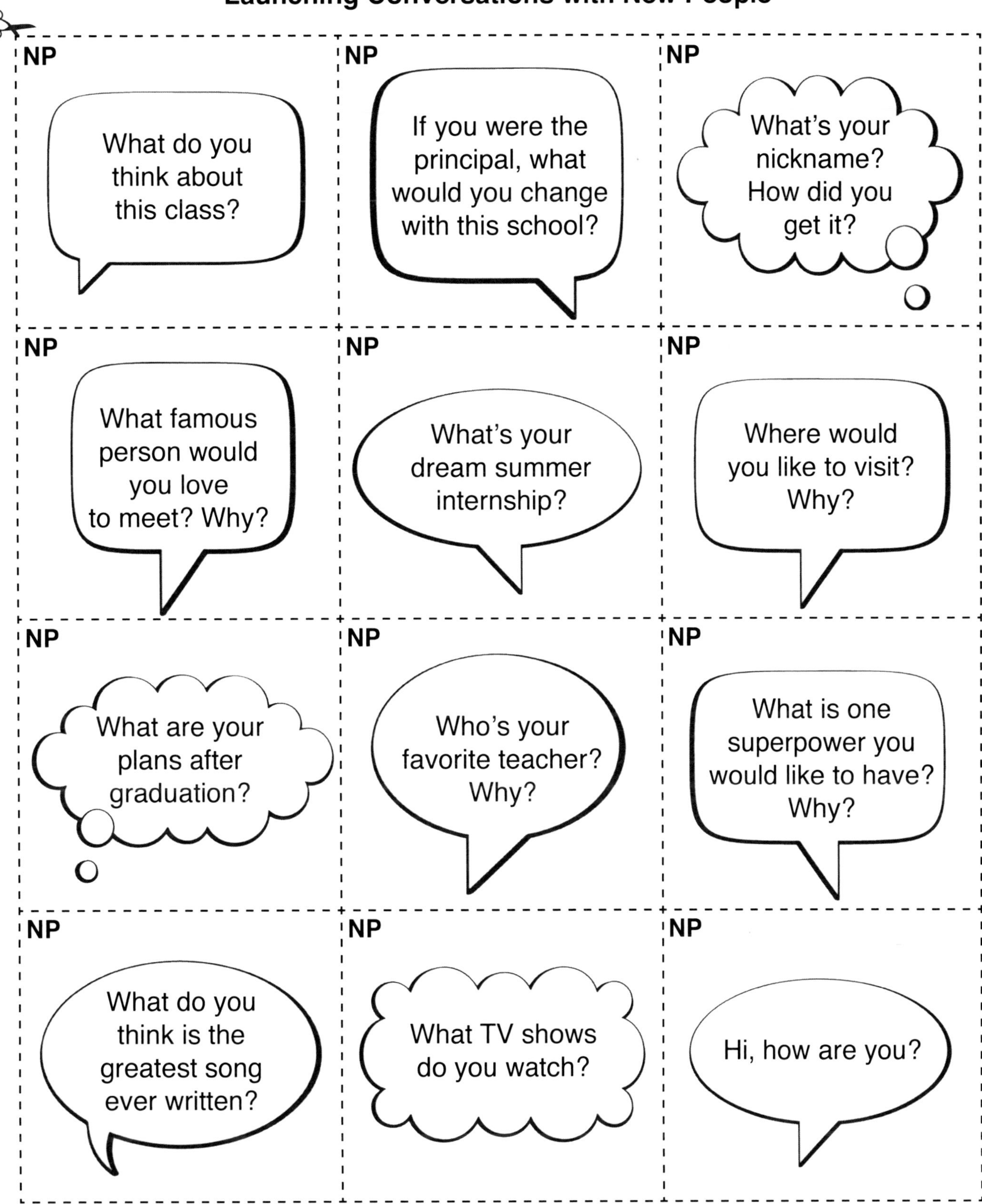

Conversations

Launching Conversations with Friends and family

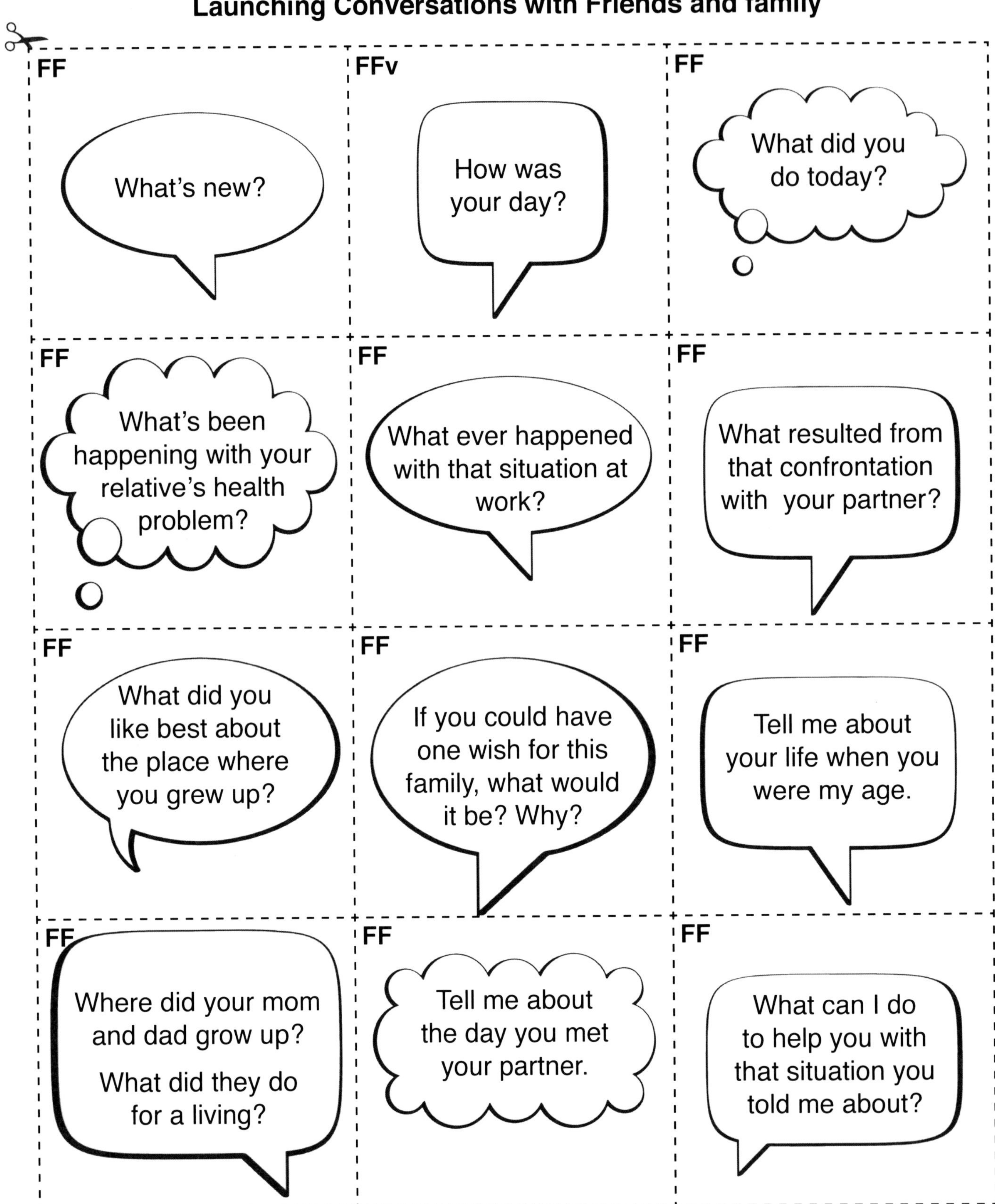

Conversations

People Joining An Ongoing Conversation

Conversations

FOR THE FACILITATOR

I. Purpose

To differentiate between questions that stimulate or stifle conversation.
To differentiate between requests to enter a conversation or rude interruptions.

II. General Comments

To practice ways to jump start and join into conversations.

III. Possible Activities

a. Before session label three containers: *New People, Friends and Family, Joiners.*
b. Photocopy the *Conversation* handout pages and cut on the broken lines.
c. Place each page's cutouts in the corresponding container.
d. The cutouts will have the following initials in the top left corner. New People – NP, Family and Friends – FF and People Joining – PJ.
e. If possible, display a balloon and ask what it means to launch a balloon (lift-off, let fly).
f. Ask what is meant by a lead balloon (a flop or failure).
g. Tell teens they will pick speech balloons that are conversation jump starters or duds.
h. Tell teens others will pick speech balloons that represent joiners or butt-ins.
i. Show teens the containers labeled *New People, Friends and Family* and *Joiners.*
j. Explain that pairs of teens take turns picking up a *New People* or *Friends and Family* cutout.
k. Pairs role play; one asks the question and the other answers as fully as possible.
l. During some of the role plays, a third teen reads a *Joiner* cutout and tries to join (or interrupt).
m. Teens retain their cutouts for later use.
n. After each role play, facilitator or teen volunteer asks the group:
   - Did *New People, Friends and Family* questions launch conversations or was it a lead balloon?
   - Did the *People Joining* questions ask permission or just butt in?
o. After all speech balloons are role played direct teens to turn over their cutouts to the blank sides.
p. Ask teens who hold speech balloons for *New People* or *Friends and Family* to compose their own speech balloons; they may write questions that stimulate or stifle conversation.
q. Ask teens who hold speech balloons for *Joiners* to compose their own questions; they may write requests to join or examples of rude interruptions.
r. Repeat the role plays with the speech balloons composed by teens.
s. Encourage teens to process the effectiveness of their questions and of the *Joiners*' efforts.

IV. Enrichment Activities

a. Encourage a discussion about how to welcome a person into a conversation.
   Possibilities
   - *Please join us.*
   - *We're discussing … What's your take on it?*
   - *Do you want to weigh in on …?*
b. Ask teens to brainstorm ways to handle someone who wants to join a private conversation.
   Possibilities
   - Encourage the person to join, but change the subject (continue the private discussion later).
   - Give up confidentiality and clue the person in on every detail (probably not desirable).
   - Say *We're sorry but this is a personal conversation.* (Safeguards the conversation but risks hurting someone's feelings).
c. Encourage a discussion of clues that tell teens not to try to join in.
   Examples
   - People are whispering or huddling.
   - One is comforting another who is crying.
   - People are arguing.

First Impressions

Likable	Unlikable
Show that you are open to meeting people.	Show disinterest for people.
Ask people about themselves.	Talk only about yourself.
Accept people's feelings.	Snicker at people's feelings.
Admit an imperfection.	Act as if you are perfect.
Share a positive outcome about something negative that happened to you.	Feel sorry for yourself.
Ask open-minded questions.	Criticize people.
Encourage people.	Brag about yourself.
Acknowledge that you hear what people say.	Act distracted and bored when people talk.
Disagree tactfully.	Argue loudly.

First Impressions

FOR THE FACILITATOR

I. Purpose

To identify actions that produce favorable or unfavorable first impressions.

II. General Comments

At a simulated party, teens enact specific behaviors and develop observational skills as they guess what others were portraying.

III. Possible Activities

a. Before session photocopy *First Impressions* handout and cut one copy on the broken lines.

b. Arrange chairs in a circle or provide a standing space, as at a party.

c. Explain that the group will pretend to meet people for the first time at a party:

- Teens will receive cutouts that describe behaviors to portray.
- Teens will **act** their parts one at a time with another person or two. They will **not** tell the reviewers what they are demonstrating.
- After the party teens will hear a list of the behaviors and will guess who portrayed each one.

d. Distribute the eighteen cutouts among participants; if more teens are present they will be observers. Observers will identify positive behaviors with notes of details and they will identify negative behaviors with notes of gestures, etc.

e. If fewer than eighteen teens are present, some teens will receive more than one cutout.

f. Suggest that teens talk about topics of interest as they would at a party and encourage teens to move around the room as they would at a party.

g. After five or ten minutes the party role play ends.

h. Read the lists aloud, one by one, and ask teens to guess who portrayed each behavior.

i. Encourage teens to share how they felt playing their parts and their reactions to peers' roles.

IV. Enrichment Activities

a. Encourage teens to discuss other positive and negative traits (honest, caring, approachable, polite, etc. or controlling, moody, insulting, insincere, etc.).

b. Encourage a discussion about people with unique clothing or hair styles (these styles suggest that people are open to new ideas and experiences, or they may want to look different from others.)

c. Encourage a discussion about language (profanity and racial jokes may offend some people).

d. Ask teens about first impressions: *Are they always accurate? Are they always lasting?* (Answers will vary).

STARTERS

Closed questions can be answered with a word or two.
Example: *How was your vacation? (Fine).*

Open-ended questions require a thoughtful, detailed response.
Example: *What happened on your trip?*

Possible topics: relationships, role models, school, sports, jobs, careers, experiences, pet peeves, concerns, improvements, emotions, schedules, priorities, money, humanitarianism, art, music, movies, books, etc.

Compose open-ended questions to start conversations and to show interest in people.

1. ______________________________
2. ______________________________
3. ______________________________
4. ______________________________
5. ______________________________
6. ______________________________
7. ______________________________
8. ______________________________
9. ______________________________
10. ______________________________

What topics are more appropriate for acquaintances?

____

____

____

What topics might open up communication with close friends and family?

____

____

____

STARTERS

FOR THE FACILITATOR

I. Purpose

To ask open-ended questions; to differentiate between sociable and more personal topics.

II. General Comments

Teens compose and ask questions in a Starter-Go-Round game.

III. Possible Activities

a. Before session coach two teens to play a parent/caregiver and student.
b. The parent/caregiver asks *How was your day?* The student responds *Okay.*
c. Actors portray the scenario when session begins; then they take their seats.
d. Ask teens what was typical about the conversation (common question and mindless answer).
e. Ask teens how a parent/caregiver might word the question differently to obtain more information. Example: Rather than saying, *What happened at school today*, say, *What was the best thing that happened at school today?*
f. Distribute the *Starters* handout; a volunteer reads aloud the information in the box.
g. Allow time for written completion.
h. Circulate among teens as they write. Coach as needed. Possible open-ended questions:
   - What qualities are most important in relationships?
   - What traits do you look for in a role model?
   - What do you like best about school?
   - What do you like least about school?
   - What do sports teach about life?
   - Tell me about your best on-the-job experience.
   - Tell me about your worst on-the-job experience.
   - What is your dream career? Why?
   - What is one of your pet peeves? Why?
   - What is your main concern about your life? Why?
   - In what ways could education (class schedules, textbooks, course offerings or the school discipline policy) be improved?
   - How might people handle jealousy?
   - What would you like to delete from your schedule? Why?
   - What is the top priority in your life right now? Why?
   - How would you spend a million dollars?
   - What types of music (or books or art or movies etc.) do you like and why?
   - To what humanitarian effort would you like to contribute? Why?

i. Elicit topics appropriate for acquaintances – school, sports, jobs, careers, schedules, money, music; for friends and family – relationships, romance, childhoods, unpleasant experiences, emotions, etc.
j. Starter-Go-Round
   - Position chairs in a circle if possible.
   - Ask teens to look at their lists to determine the best questions to ask peers.
   - Explain if people are uncomfortable with a topic they may ask for a different question.
   - Teens ask questions from their lists to the person on their right (who answers).
   - Next, the teens who answered questions will ask questions from their lists to the persons on their left (who answers).

IV. Enrichment Activities

Encourage teens to ask open-ended questions outside of group and report back about the effectiveness of their conversation starters.

Stoppers

Topper – Whatever bad happened to someone, something happened to me that was worse.

Interrupter – What I have to say is most important, so I butt in and blurt out.

Advisor – I know best what people should or shouldn't do, and I say so!

Monopolizer – I wait my turn then talk non-stop, usually it's all about me and no one can get a word in.

Subject Changer – I don't care what others discuss, I abruptly bring up what I want to talk about.

Gossiper – I talk about people behind their backs.

Know-It-All – I'm an expert on any topic. Just ask me!

Challenger – Whatever others believe, I disagree.

Snooper – I ask personal questions that are none of my business.

Instigator – I bring up controversial topics like religion and politics, insult people or start conflict.

Stoppers

FOR THE FACILITATOR

I. Purpose

To identify and avoid using conversation stoppers.

II. General Comments

Through a role-play game, teens portray annoying social behaviors to illustrate what not to do.

III. Possible Activities

a. Before session photocopy the *Stoppers* handout and cut on the broken lines.
b. Place the cut-outs face down in a stack.
c. Ten teens volunteer to pick up a cut-out and role play a behavior.
d. If there are fewer than ten volunteers, use one cut-out per volunteer for the first *round*; then repeat the game with remaining cut-outs the next *round*. If more than ten are present, after the first ten participants have completed their role play the others can choose one of the cutouts they would like to role-play in a different way.
e. Tell teens that players have *secret* conversation stopper identities; they do not divulge their roles to other players or observers
f. Encourage teens to decide on a topic of interest (favorite foods, music, movies, pets; most embarrassing moments; peak experiences; where to go on a first date; school rule revisions; issues with parents or bosses; childhood best friends; whatever is relevant).
g. List the *stopper* names on the board.
h. Players sit in the front of the room or near each other in the circle and portray their roles as they talk.
i. After a few minutes players and/or observers guess *stoppers*' identities.
j. Ask teens ways *stoppers* might change.

Examples

- Toppers can compliment others or comment on others' accomplishments or challenges.
- Interrupters can focus on what is being said rather than what they want to say.
- Advisors can ask people what they have tried before or what options they have.
- Monopolizers can purposely speak briefly, listen and ask questions.
- Subject Changers can stick to the topic or wait for a lull in the conversation.
- Gossipers can decide to be nice or say nothing at all.
- Know-It-Alls can decide they know less or keep their brilliance to themselves.
- Challengers can share opinions but not try to convince others.
- Snoopers can respect privacy and avoid questions that make people uncomfortable.
- Instigators can learn if, what and when controversial subjects are appropriate.

IV. Enrichment Activities

Encourage teens to brainstorm other *Dialogue Don'ts* while a peer lists ideas on the board.

Possibilities

- Don't talk about disgusting topics, especially when people are eating.
- Don't say, text, e-mail or post anything you don't want the world to see.
- Don't bully.
- Don't degrade or label groups of people.
- Don't tell secrets (unless they involve harm to self, others, abuse or addiction.) A trusted adult needs to know this information.
- Don't tell off-color jokes or jokes that demean particular types of people.

Pushover to Assertor

Pushovers (passive people) become doormats, allowing others to trample on their rights. They do not voice their own needs, wants or opinions and have a problem saying *No*.

In these situations, what would a *pushover* do?

1. As a pushover is driving, friends indulge in illegal substances.
2. A dating partner pressures a pushover to have sex. The pushover doesn't want to.
3. Friends ask a pushover to distract the cashier while they shoplift.
4. A friend asks a pushover to do his/her homework.
5. A pushover is abused and told not to tell anyone.
6. A pushover's parents or caregivers criticize the pushover's career goals.
7. Someone makes a hurtful comment to a pushover.

Aggressors (aggressive people) blame, control, dominate, bully and humiliate. They do not respect others' rights.

In these situations what would an aggressor do?

8. Someone gives an aggressor a dirty look.
9. A caregiver says *No* to an aggressor's request.
10. A former friend gossips about an aggressor.
11. A dating partner breaks up with an aggressor.
12. A teacher or boss criticizes an aggressor.
13. An aggressor is wrongly accused.
14. An aggressor says he/she is angry and someone challenges him/her to do something about it.

Manipulators (manipulative people) are passive-aggressive and pretend to be pleasant but plot to get even. They seem agreeable and then sabotage people behind their backs.

In these situations what would a manipulator do?

15. A friend asks a manipulator to help at a fundraiser car wash; the manipulator would rather not.
16. A manipulator plans an acting career; the theater instructor picks someone else for the lead role.
17. A sports teammate performs better than a manipulator.
18. A caregiver refuses to loan money to a manipulator.
19. The manipulator's dating partner flirts with someone else.
20. A manipulator feels ignored or insignificant.
21. A manipulator receives incorrect change (ten dollars too much) from a fast food cashier.

Assertors (assertive people) clearly state honest, open and direct opinions and feelings. They stick up for their own rights and needs without violating others' rights.

In these situations what would an assertor do?

22. A friend drove an assertor to a party and got drunk. The assertor is afraid to ride back home.
23. An older relative makes sexual advances to an assertor. The assertor's parents don't believe it.
24. An assertor is being blackmailed to pay money or the blackmailer will share a private photo.
25. A boy/girlfriend continually borrows money from an assertor without paying it back.
26. A friend invites an assertor to go swimming. The assertor doesn't know how to swim.
27. A neighbor asks an assertor a favor. The assertor has prior plans.
28. Peers or friends ask personal questions the assertor does not want to answer.

Pushover to Assertor

FOR THE FACILITATOR

I. Purpose

To differentiate among passive, aggressive, passive-aggressive and assertive responses.

II. General Comments

Teens identify socially acceptable ways to meet needs and maintain individual rights.

III. Possible Activities

a. Write on the board the following terms and elicit definitions (possibilities are parenthesized): **Pushovers** (weak, give in to everyone); passive; **Aggressors** (fight physically or verbally); **Manipulators** (passive-aggressive) **Assertors** (advocate for their own rights and needs).
b. A game show host sits at the front of the room and receives the *Pushover to Assertor* handout.
c. Peer players take turns selecting a category and responding to the questions read by the host.
d. Players share a possible consequence or reward. Examples correspond to question numbers:

The Pushover …

1. Lets them; gets pulled over by police with illegal substances in the vehicle.
2. Give in; is sorry; feels used and/or worries about a disease or pregnancy.
3. Keeps the cashier busy; gets busted as a partner in the crime.
4. Does the homework; wonders if this is a true friend; worries about getting caught.
5. Suffers in fear and silence; abuse gets worse.
6. Listens to concerns; disagrees but gives up dream; always wonders What if …
7. Feelings are hurt; says nothing; builds up anger or isolates to prevent future put-downs.

The Aggressor …

8. Gives a dirtier look; situation worsens.
9. Slams doors; throws things; call the person names; the door to further discussion is closed.
10. Gossips even more; other people add fuel to the flame.
11. Says mean things orally and electronically; damages everyone's reputations.
12. Lashes out loudly in class or workplace; makes threats; faces disciplinary action.
13. Swears, name-calls, punches walls; rather than being cleared, looks more like trouble.
14. Throws a punch; the fight worsens; people get hurt and legal problems result.

The Manipulator …

15. Says *I'll be there* but never shows up; friend loses trust.
16. Congratulates the person but whispers about his/her poor acting ability; jealousy shows.
17. Spreads a lie that the person uses steroids; gets in trouble for false accusations.
18. Steals caregiver's money; gets caught; does not get caught (yet) and continues to steal.
19. Flirts with that person's partner; doesn't clarify the relationship status with partner.
20. Falls down or says he/she is seriously sick to gain sympathy; can be found out.
21. Keeps the extra money; later feels guilty and doesn't enjoy spending the cash.

The Assertor …

22. Tells friend he/she is not safe to drive; finds a safe way home; arrives home intact.
23. Tells a trusted teacher or counselor; the abuser is stopped; assertor feels empowered, not victimized.
24. Does not pay; tells a trusted adult; blackmailer is stopped.
25. Lends no more money; relationship continues; if the person leaves, it is better to know now.
26. Admits inability to swim; says *I would like to learn*; goes and has fun watching.
27. States having other plans; sticks to agenda; may offer to help at another time.
28. Says *Thanks for caring but I'd rather not talk about it*; maintains privacy.

IV. Enrichment Activities

Ask teens to brainstorm their personal rights, those that do not infringe on others' rights.

Negotiation Know-How

Use the example below to help you role play and in the future, be able to apply it to real life.

Your parent/caregiver asks you to stay off the computer; you know a problem is coming.

Your Words	Your Parent / Caregiver's Possible Responses
Set a time: *What would be a good time to talk?*	*After dinner.*
Ask the person's point of view: *What are your concerns?*	*You don't seem to ever finish your homework.*
Reflect: *Are you worried about my grades?*	*Yes, your grades have been falling.*
Share your needs: *It's important to me to stay connected to my friends.*	*And, it's important to me that you graduate.*
Brainstorm options: *I could do homework one hour; then contact friends.* *I could text and blog while studying.* *I could ask for peer tutoring.*	*You could do homework six hours each day, or you could turn off your cell phone during that time, or you could use your computer for school projects only.*
Select win-win possibilities: *I'm willing to turn phone off during homework time.* *I'm willing to use computer for school and socializing.*	*I'm fine with turning off your phone for six hours of homework each day.* *I'm fine with social networking after six hours of homework.*
Select the best or compromise: *Let's set a schedule.* *I want one hour of homework; you want six.* *What about three?*	*Let's try three hours of school work with phone turned off and then socialize.*
Develop a plan of action: *Let's start today.*	*If your grades go up, we'll stick with the schedule; if not we'll re-negotiate.*

Tips to deal with confrontational or competitive types of people

- If your needs are attacked, ask about the person's feelings and reasons. (Discover motivations).
- If your ideas are attacked, encourage criticism and advice. (You'll learn more about their concerns).
- If you are verbally attacked say *Let's stick to the issue.* (It's not about personalities or power).
- Silence may help. (Used sparingly, silence lets the person re-think; the person may suggest a solution).
- Avoid angry or prideful reactions. (Keep your tone calm, level and cooperative).
- If efforts fail, consult a neutral third party. (Both agree in advance to accept the person's suggestions).

Negotiation Know-How

FOR THE FACILITATOR

I. Purpose

To practice negotiation, an essential social skill in adolescence and adulthood.

II. General Comments

Teens learn to bargain and compromise in a collaborative rather than competitive style.

III. Possible Activities

a. Write these categories on the board in columns: Parents/Caregivers, Friends, Dating Partners, Employers or Volunteer Supervisors.

b. Ask teens to brainstorm possible areas of disagreement as a peer lists ideas on board.
Possibilities

Parents/Caregivers	Friends	Dating Partners	Employers or Volunteer Supervisors
Dating Friends Household chores Appearance Family issues	Loyalty Where to go What to do Borrowing What to wear	Sexuality Level of commitment Respect Confidentiality Loyalty	Schedules Duties Co-worker issues Pay raises & appreciation Improving conditions

c. Ask teens to add different categories if they wish.

d. Explain that teens will negotiate to get what they want and compromise for a *win-win.*

e. Distribute the *Negotiation Know-How* handout; a teen reads the examples aloud.

f. Ask teens the rationales for each step; ideas to elicit are parenthesized:
- Set a time. (Not in the heat of anger or when people are rushed or preoccupied).
- Ask the person's point of view. (The person speaks first; then you know their motivations).
- Reflect. (You prove you have listened and understand).
- Share your needs. (You listened first; You hope the person will be receptive to your side).
- Brainstorm options. (Think together about creative, yet practical possibilities).
- Select win-win possibilities. (Some options are okay with both people).
- Select the best or compromise. (Find mutually acceptable middle ground).
- Develop a plan of action. (Decide how both will know whether the plan works).

g. Teens pair up with peers and prepare to play parent/caregiver and teen, two friends, dating partners or employer and employee; they briefly decide on an issue that causes conflict.

h. Remind teens to refer to the steps on their handouts as they plan their role plays.

i. The group re-convenes; teens take turns role playing the steps in front of peers (audience).

j. Teens may refer to their handouts as they go through the steps; audience gives feedback.

k. Set time limits for the performances (three to five minutes).

l. After everyone has had a turn, teens read aloud and discuss the tips at the bottom of the page.

IV. Enrichment Activity

a. Encourage a discussion of barriers to successful negotiation. Ideas to elicit:
- The need to win at all costs
- Refusal to give an inch
- Unwillingness to see the other person's perspective
- Blame and/or power struggles
- Inhibitions during brainstorming which squelch creative solutions

b. Encourage teens to use the handout in real situations and report outcomes to the group.

EXPECTATIONS 2

We tend to live up to our expectations.

~ Earl Nightingale

Tic-Tac-Tech

1. Name a place **not** to talk on a cell phone.
2. Tell something **not** to do on a cell phone.
3. In what situation should cell phones be turned off or set on *vibrate*?
4. When on a speakerphone, what do you need to do at the start of the conversation?
5. Why move away from a group of people when you are talking on your phone?
6. What is the problem with a long song or greeting on your voice mail?
7. When you leave a voice mail, what three pieces of info should you give?
8. How do most people react to long, rambling messages left on voice mail?
9. What types of messages are better given in person?
10. It is deadly to text when ______________________.
11. How do you feel when someone you are with texts or talks on the cell phone?
12. What is the problem with slang and abbreviations in texts?
13. Why is it unrealistic to expect immediate responses from your text or voice mail messages?
14. Why turn off the TV or music when you're on the phone?
15. Why decline to forward an email that says "Forward to 10 people"?
16. You have a cold. What should you do after speaking on a phone that others also use?
17. When people visit, what needs to happen to the TV or music?
18. When watching TV with others, what types of food-related noises should one avoid?
19. Why refrain from flipping around channels during commercials when people are watching TV?
20. What behavior annoys others during a program or TV movie?
21. What question do you need to ask yourself before sending emails or posting on sites?
22. People expect email responses immediately. You need more time. What should you do?
23. What action is advisable before you send long attachments or lots of photos?
24. Before sending political or controversial content, what do you need to know?
25. Why not use a silly email address?
26. What info should not be given as you email or post about your upcoming vacation?
27. What message is conveyed when you use all capital letters in an email?
28. Why not give personal info to someone you think you know in a chat room?
29. Why not use sarcasm or jokes in texts?
30. What's wrong with emails that are all about you?
31. When is it okay to forward other people's messages?
32. You receive an angry email. What's your best first action?
33. In addition to friends and family, who might see your posts, photos, emails?
34. What's best to do if you post messages on someone's site or send a few emails with no response?
35. How might social media sites and email help a shy person?
36. Give two reasons to limit your time online.
37. How might social media interfere with social skill development?
38. Why are greetings like *Hello Bob* and closings like *Thank you* needed in emails?
39. Why is it necessary to state your subject in the subject line of an email?
40. What very important part of communication is missing from technological messages?

See accompanying page, *Tic-Tac-Tech Examples for Game Show Host or Facilitator*, page 37.

Tic-Tac-Tech

FOR THE FACILITATOR

I. Purpose

To consider technology-related manners.

II. General Comments

Teens spend increasing time and energy on cell phones, computers and other electronic devices. Excessive social networking may impede interpersonal interaction and skill development.

III. Possible Activities

a. Write *Tic-Tac-Tech* on the board and draw a diagram on the board.

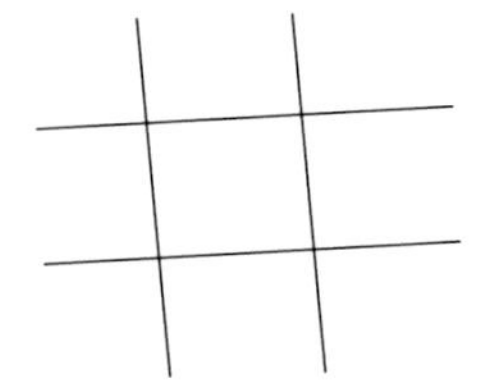

b. Ask teens to guess what the session is about (a game related to technology).
c. A volunteer game show host sits near the front of the room.
d. Host receives the *Tic-Tac-Tech* questions and *Examples* (possible responses) handouts.
e. Teens divide into teams and sit on different sides of the room; the *X-Team* and the *O-Team*.
f. Label each side of the board *X-Team* and *O-Team*; list members' names or captains under each.
g. Host asks questions of alternate teams; members may collaborate on answers.
h. As a team answers acceptably, a member places and X or O on the game board.
i. Team members may add other responses. (no extra points)
j. Host or facilitator decides which responses are reasonable; the examples are guidelines only.
k. Host or a scorekeeper records the number of wins for each team underneath their names.
l. A team wins when its letters fill a horizontal, vertical or diagonal row.
m. If no team fills a row, the team with the most letters on the board wins that round.
n. Erase and begin a new game with a new host as each round is completed.
o. The team with the most winning rounds is the winner.

IV. Enrichment Activities

a. Ask teens to share feelings about rude technological actions they have encountered.
b. Ask teens to brainstorm consequences of misused technology.

Possibilities

- It is permanent and can be used against you; if you bully online, the evidence can prove your guilt.
- Sexually explicit photos can be considered violations of privacy or child pornography.
- Adult predators can locate and harm anyone who divulges identifying information.
- Sexting allows images to be seen by everyone; damaged reputation and embarrassment have led to depression and suicidal thoughts and actions.
- Friends today may be enemies tomorrow and may spread photos and revelations you thought were forever confidential.
- Your actions and opinions may change but they stay to haunt you and to harm you and others for years to come.

Tic-Tac-Tech

Examples for Game Show Host or Facilitator

Accept any reasonable responses. Possible answers and concepts to elicit:

1. On dates or at gatherings where family/friends are present who would like your full attention.
2. Argue, gossip, bully, send private photos or texts.
3. Religious services, classes, meetings, concerts, theaters; wherever ringtones would distract.
4. Notify the person with whom you speak and all people present in the room.
5. Avoid disturbing others; safeguard your privacy.
6. Listeners often have limited time and/or patience,
7. Your name (even if you think the person knows your voice), phone number and reason for call.
8. Annoyance, don't listen to full message; long messages fill up people's voice mail quicker.
9. Any negative news like a break-up or conflict-related issues.
10. Driving; also doing any activity that requires your full attention like operating machinery.
11. Ignored and insignificant.
12. Recipient might not understand the message.
13. People are busy and may have other priorities.
14. Background noise may irritate or distract people.
15. Original sender will use these emails for advertisements, etc.
16. Use a disinfectant wipe or spray on the phone.
17. Turn it off.
18. Noisy foods, cellophane wrappers, and do not clang metal utensils on bowls.
19. You might not return to the program on time, people miss important parts.
20. Talking, predicting the ending, finding flaws
21. *Is it okay for the world to see this?* Once sent, it cannot be erased, it's indelible forever.
22. Send a message explaining your usual response time.
23. Ask first.
24. Know your recipient(s); they may hold different beliefs and/or be offended.
25. College admission counselors, prospective employers or others might be turned off.
26. The dates you will be out of town.
27. SHOUTING at people.
28. The person may use the info to harm you.
29. People might not understand how you meant it.
30. People tire of self-centered content; ask appropriate questions about their lives.
31. Info and photos you receive are private; it's unethical and possibly illegal to forward to others without permission.
32. Cool down, take your time, do not respond in anger; ideally ask to talk in person.
33. Everyone; people may use them against you to cyber-bully, cyber-stalk or for other abusive purposes.
34. Stop, they clearly are not interested.
35. Shy people are more comfortable with more time to think about what to write.
36. Life (exercise, attend events, etc.); your activities will make your posts more interesting.
37. Too little face-to-face communication where you can see the other person's facial expressions, hear the tone of voice or see the look in the person's eyes.
38. They are polite in electronic or hard copy communication.
39. It tells recipients the topic of your email; people prioritize accordingly.
40. Non-verbal communication like facial expression and body language.

Tic-Tac-Tech

FOR THE FACILITATOR *(Continued from page 38)*

IV. Enrichment Activities

c. Write quotes on the board, one at a time or distribute copies of this page to participants to use as "homework."

d. Encourage teens to interpret and personalize each.

You are what you share. ~ Charles Leadbeater

Focus on how to be social; not how to do social. ~ Jay Baer

Our social tools are not an improvement to modern society; they are a challenge to it. ~ Clay Shirkey

Munch Match

Use the top half of page for the interactive game or individual puzzle.

Napkin	Lap	Last piece of food	Ask first
Chew	Mouth closed	Salt	Taste first
Talk	Pleasant topics	Fast or slow eater	Pace yourself
Bites	Small	Slurp	Eat quietly
Double dip	Never	Toothpick	Use in the restroom
Something too chewy	Spit into napkin	Hot food	Wait a while
Phones, electronics	Do not use	Tip	15-20%
Blow nose	Leave the table	Spill on someone	Do not touch
Utensils	Use them!	Keys, belongings	Do not put them on the table
Reach	"Please pass the …"	Someone doesn't eat	Don't comment

Use the bottom half of page for individual or team matching exercise.

Munch Match

1. Napkin
2. Chew
3. Talk
4. Bites
5. Double dip
6. Something too chewy
7. Phones, electronics
8. Blow nose
9. Utensils
10. Reach
11. Last piece of food
12. Salt
13. Fast or slow eater
14. Slurp
15. Toothpick
16. Hot food
17. Tip
18. Spill on someone
19. Keys, belongings
20. Someone doesn't eat

A. Pleasant topics
B. Never
C. Spit into napkin
D. Do not touch
E. Use them!
F. "Please pass the …"
G. Mouth closed
H. Pace yourself
I. Eat quietly
J. Leave the table
K. Use in the restroom
L. Wait a while
M. 15-20%
N. Lap
O. Do not put them on the table
P. Don't comment
Q. Small
R. Taste first
S. Do not use
T. Ask first

Munch Match

FOR THE FACILITATOR

I. Purpose

To make reviewing table manner topics fun; to raise awareness of socially acceptable behavior.

II. General Comments

Although dining is often casual and rules are relaxed, teens need to know the basics.

III. Possible Activities

a. Before session ask a male and female to volunteer for a brief mock video.
b. Use an empty cup and napkin as props; coach teens to portray this scenario:
    As they eat and drink the male spills liquid onto the female's torso.
    He is about to wipe the liquid off with his napkin, then freezes before he touches her.
c. Ask the group what he should do (apologize, and offer to pay the cleaning bill).
d. Ask why he would not wipe up the spill (inappropriate touching).
e. Explain that the session's topic relates to dos and don'ts regarding food.
f. Draw two squares on the board; write *Mouth full* in one and *Don't talk* in the other.
g. Explain that these terms are a match because we should not talk with our mouths full.

1. **Interactive Game – Use the top half of the handout.**
    - Before session photocopy the *Munch Match* handout, cut on the broken lines; mix pieces up.
    - Divide the forty pieces of paper as evenly as possible among all teens.
    - Teens take turns reading aloud one of their terms and asking who might have the match.
    - A person who might have a match reads the cutout and states how the terms are related. Example: A teen reads aloud *Napkin*; whoever has *Lap* will identify that they have the match because napkins are put in laps.
    - Some teens may have picked matching cutouts and will share about them.
    - The answer key is the uncut *Munch Match* page: the first and second columns are pairs; the third and fourth columns are pairs.
    - Teens put used cutouts face down and continue to play until all cutouts are matched.
2. **Individual Puzzle – Use the top half of the handout.**
    - Before session make enough copies of the handout for each teen; cut on the broken lines.
    - Keep each page of cutouts separate as each teen receives a scrambled set of forty.
    - Teens look for matching cutouts and set each pair aside until they have twenty.
    - After completion, teens share about their pairs and why they believe they match.
    - The answer key is the uncut *Munch Match* page: the first and second columns are pairs; the third and fourth columns are pairs.
3. **Individual or Team Matching Exercise – Use the bottom half of the handout.**
    - Distribute the handout to individual teens or teams; allow time for completion.
    - Teens share responses and reasons i.e. *Napkin* matches *Lap* because it is placed on lap.
    - Answers:
      1-N, 2-G, 3-A, 4-Q, 5-B, 6-C, 7-S, 8-J, 9-E, 10-F, 11-T
      12-R, 13-H, 14-I, 15-K, 16-L, 17-M, 18-D, 19-O, 20-P

IV. Enrichment Activities

a. Encourage a discussion of whether the expectations discussed in the activity are ridiculous or old-fashioned rules, or common sense, and explain why.
b. Ask teens to identify other socially acceptable or unacceptable practices.
c. Ask teens to brainstorm their own sets of *munch matches*.

Edit Your Intros

Teacher in the Aisle

You're in a store with your friend Brandon and your history teacher shows up in your aisle.
You say *Brandon, this is my history teacher Mrs. Levi. Mrs. Levi, this is my friend Brandon Jones.*

Grandpa Jones' Birthday

Your friend Ashley accompanies you to your grandfather's birthday party. You say *Grandpa, this is my friend Ashley Smith. Ashley this is my grandpa, Fred Jones.* Ashley says *Glad to meet you Grampa.*

Restaurant Meeting

You are sitting in a restaurant with your friend. Your friend introduces you an older person.
You say to the older person, from your chair, *"I'm glad to meet you.*

New Student

A new student joins you at lunch.
You say *Nick, Alyssa and Tyler, this is a new student Chris Chapman. Chris, these are my friends.*

Parent or Care-Provider and Coach

Your parent or care-provider attends your game. You are with your coach after the game.
You say, *Mom, this is my coach Mr. Johnson. Mr. Johnson, this is my mom Maria Martinez.*

Two Acquaintances

You introduce two of your friends and state their names.
Then you say *Please shake hands and get to know each other.*

Neighbor and Aunt

You introduce your adult neighbor to your aunt and state their names.
Then you say *You two have a lot in common. You both suffer from arthritis.*

Date at a Party

You are at a party with your dating partner. A student from your school does not know your partner.
You forgot the student's name so you say *Hi, how are you?* You tell your partner *He goes to my school.*

Edit Your Intros

FOR THE FACILITATOR

I. Purpose

To learn and practice introduction basics through mock videos or in an individual activity format.

II. General Comments

Introduction skills are critical in social and professional encounters throughout life.

III. Possible Activities

1. Video Format

a. Before session photocopy the *Edit Your Intros* handout and cut on the broken lines; put cutout scripts into a container; groups of three to five teens will take turns role playing.
b. Ask teens how many have visited a video-sharing website and/or have made their own videos.
c. Explain that casts of three to five actors will pretend to make a video (act while the audience watches); they will take turns portraying introductions.
d. Explain that the audience will find the flaws which relate to social expectations (or manners).
e. Explain that the actors will then re-enact the scene correctly.
f. The scenarios require three actors except for *New Student* which requires five.
g. For each scenario, actors go to the front of the room; one pulls a cutout script from the container.
h. Actors briefly huddle to decide on roles; the actor(s) with speaking parts hold or share scripts.
i. They perform; audience tries to detect the social error in each; the actors re-do the scene correctly.
j. Provide help for teens to find the social flaws.

Ideas to elicit and correct re-enactments:

Teacher in Aisle – When introducing, say the name of the older person or the person with the higher rank first. *Mrs. Levi, this is my friend Brandon Jones. Mrs. Levi is my history teacher.*

Grandpa Jones's Birthday – Ashley is expected to show respect and says *Glad to meet you Mr. Jones.*

Restaurant Meeting – A young person stands when introduced to an older person.

New Student – Say an individual's name first; then name members of a group. *Chris, these are my friends Nick, Alyssa and Tyler. Everybody, this is Chris."*

Care-Provider and Coach – Say the coach's name first. *Mr. Johnson, this is my mom, Maria Martinez. Mom, Mr. Johnson is my coach.*

Two Acquaintances – Do not tell people to shake hands; state something they might have in common, to stimulate conversation. *You both have an interest in art.*

Neighbor and Aunt – Do not mention diseases. Mention they have some things in common.

Date at a Party – Admit you have forgotten a name. *I'm sorry I forgot your name;* the person identifies himself as Tyler. Say your date's name first (you have known her longer). *Kaylee, this is Tyler from my school. Kaylee is my girlfriend.*

2. Individual Activity

a. Distribute the handout uncut and ask teens to find the social expectation flaw in each scenario.
b. Teens write their suggested corrections on a separate paper; encourage teens to share their responses.

IV. Enrichment Activities

Encourage a discussion about how to handle handshakes.

Elicit concepts

- The person with higher rank extends hand first; i.e. a job interviewer would initiate a handshake.
- Do not extend your hand to someone whose right hand or arm is injured or needed for a cane or crutches; avoid extending your hand if a person's hands are being used to carry books, packages, etc.
- Practice shaking hands, firmly but not too firmly.

Social Savant
Event Team Questions

1. You received a gift for a special occasion and you said thank you in person.
    a. Send a text thank you note.
    b. Send an email thank you note.
    c. Send a handwritten thank you note.
2. At a graduation party you use the last paper towel.
    a. Say nothing.
    b. Rummage through cabinets to find more towels.
    c. Quietly tell the host.
3. When you thank people for a money gift …
    a. State the exact amount of money.
    b. Say you wish it was more.
    c. Mention the person's generosity.
4. For your grandmother's birthday party …
    a. You tell your parents or caregiver to add your name to the card.
    b. You think, because you're a teen, you don't need to bring either a card or gift.
    c. You bring a card, purchased or handmade.
5. You're going to a school dance with a date.
    a. You tell your family you'll be home at 11 and come home later without calling.
    b. You tell your family you'll be home at 11, but sleep at someone else's house without calling.
    c. You tell your family you'll be home at 11 and will call if you'll be late, and you do.
6. You're invited to your latest girl/boyfriend's home for dinner the first time.
    a. You arrive late.
    b. You arrive on time with a small gift (flowers, a small plant, sweets).
    c. You arrive on time and sit at the table without offering to help.
7. You go to the movies with a group of friends.
    a. You all walk in after the movie started, making noise as you look for seats.
    b. You talk during the movie.
    c. You arrive early so you can all sit together, do your talking before and after the movie.
8. You go to an orchestra's classical music concert.
    a. You come late and insist on the usher letting you in during the music.
    b. You clap between movements (sections) of the symphony.
    c. You arrive on time and wait for the conductor to put the baton down before applauding.
9. Your aunt invites you out for lunch and meets you at the restaurant.
    a. You bring an uninvited guest with you.
    b. You offer to help with the bill or offer to pay the tip.
    c. You leave before the bill arrives.
10. When invited to a wedding …
    a. You respond to the RSVP to say you will attend.
    b. You wait until the last minute to decide and just show up.
    c. You take a couple of friends with you.
11. At a wedding service
    a. You leave as soon as the bride and groom are out the door.
    b. You leave when your cell phone ringtone goes off.
    c. You leave after the families of the bride and groom leave.
12. At a religious service
    a. You come late and walk all the way to the front to sit with someone you know.
    b. You stand and sit when everyone else does.
    c. You make remarks when a clergy person is speaking.

Social Savant
Travel Team Questions

1. You are in a line waiting for a bus, train or airplane.
    a. Fumble to find your ID and boarding pass or ticket.
    b. Have your information readily available.
    c. Ask people to save your place as you run to your car for your license.
2. On the day of your trip …
    a. Wear heavy cologne in a scent you love.
    b. Eat onions or garlic before you board.
    c. Shower and wear clean clothes.
3. A family with elderly members and toddlers are in line in front of you.
    a. Smile and ask if you can help.
    b. Mumble to people behind you to be prepared for a long delay.
    c. Give the family dirty looks.
4. You want to sleep on the trip.
    a. Recline your seat when drowsiness hits you.
    b. Sleep straight up.
    c. Look behind before you recline to be sure you don't knock over food or drink.
5. A child sitting behind you is kicking your seat.
    a. Tell the child to stop.
    b. Ask the parent to tell the child to stop.
    c. Complain to an authority.
6. What are the unwritten rules for arm rests between seats?
    a. Use it first and you own it for the trip.
    b. Always leave arm rests for the next person.
    c. Outer arm rests are for aisle or window seats and the middle ones are for the middle person.
7. The person next to you is reading.
    a. Ask about the person's taste in literature.
    b. Let the person read.
    c. Talk about your favorite book.
8. A person next to you is squeezing past you to go to the restroom.
    a. Sit still.
    b. Move your legs to the side.
    c. Stand until the person passes by.
9. When the trip ends …
    a. Quickly open the overhead bin to retrieve your belongings.
    b. Carefully open the overhead bin to retrieve your belongings.
    c. Forget to retrieve your belongings until you are half way down the aisle.
10. You are about to get on a bus.
    a. Let people get off first, then board the bus.
    b. You go first.
    c. Take turns, one person steps off and one steps on, etc.
11. An elderly person enters a bus or train and there is standing room only.
    a. Let the person stand.
    b. Tell someone younger than you to give up his/her seat.
    c. Offer your seat.
12. When you see friends after the trip …
    a. Impress them with lots of stories about your vacation.
    b. Show lots of photos.
    c. Briefly *show and tell* about the trip if asked.

Social Savant

Condolence Team Questions

1. Someone you know died.
   a. You call the family and ask the cause of death.
   b. You call the family and ask how you can help.
   c. You send an email or text to say you are sorry.
2. You are at a funeral service but don't understand what is happening.
   a. You ask someone next to you during the service.
   b. Later, you ask someone who is not a family member.
   c. You make a guess and then share it with your friends.
3. After a funeral service …
   a. You speak to the family first.
   b. You rush in and comfort your friends.
   c. You talk about embarrassing moments you shared with the deceased to lighten the mood.
4. At a funeral …
   a. You dress conservatively but you need not wear black.
   b. You must wear black to show you mourn the dead.
   c. You wear your newest most stylish outfit to show respect.
5. You visit the family after the funeral.
   a. Stay a long time and only talk with your friends.
   b. You share a nice story about the deceased person with the family.
   c. Ask if there was a life insurance policy to cover their costs.
6. Which is better to say to the deceased person's family?
   a. I know how you feel.
   b. I'm sorry for your loss.
   c. It's for the best.
7. You hear a story about how the deceased person died and don't know if it's true.
   a. You pass on the story to everyone you talk with.
   b. You ask the closest relative.
   c. You say nothing and wait until official information comes out.
8. You are in a funeral receiving line and don't know the family.
   a. You say nothing.
   b. You say your name and how you know the deceased person.
   c. You leave the line.
9. Your good friend's parent dies.
   a. You attend the funeral only.
   b. You say you're sorry and nothing else.
   c. You let your friend know that you are available if he/she needs to talk.
10. At the home of the family, you don't know anyone.
    a. You introduce yourself to the relatives.
    b. You just find something to eat.
    c. You leave.
11. When someone dies out of town, it is most important to …
    a. Send a donation.
    b. Send a card.
    c. Send flowers.
12. What is appropriate at a family's home after a death?
    a. Text, facebook, tweet.
    b. Take a cell phone call.
    c. Be respectful, speak in low tones and express condolences to the family.

Social Savant

FOR THE FACILITATOR

I. Purpose

To highlight social graces related to events, condolences and travel, by using the term savant, which means a wise person.

II. General Comments

Although most teens know what is right, the game reinforces consideration and courtesy.

III. Possible Activities

a. Teens split into three teams: Events, Travel and Condolence.
b. Host alternately reads questions to each team.

Event	Answer	EVENT - Correct Responses with Rationale
1.	c	Handwritten notes are respectful; electronics are too impersonal.
2.	c	The host will replace the towels; do not look through cabinets.
3.	c	Thank people for their generosity; you may say what the funds will be used for.
4.	c	It will be most meaningful to bring your own card or make one yourself.
5.	c	Be responsible and keep your promise.
6.	b	A small gift, being on time and helping will be impressive!
7.	c	Consideration of others in the movies is a mature way of behaving.
8.	c	Respect to the orchestra and audience is important.
9.	b	You will be acknowledged as a grown up by offering to contribute.
10.	a	Respond in a timely manner and never take uninvited guests.
11.	c	The family leaves first. Your cell phone would be off.
12.	b	Unless it goes against your religion, be respectful by doing what everyone else does.

Event	Answer	TRAVEL - Correct Responses with Rationale
1.	b	Have your paperwork in hand to speed up the process.
2.	c	Others may be allergic to your cologne; be clean and have fresh breath.
3.	a	Show empathy for elders and have patience with children.
4.	c	Look first; ideally ask the person behind you if you may recline your seat.
5.	b	Ask the parent before speaking to an authority; don't reprimand someone's child.
6.	c	The person in the middle deserves the middle arm rests.
7.	b	Respect a person's right to read or preference for solitude.
8.	c	To stand gives the person the most space to get past you.
9.	b	Be careful that items do not fly or fall out of the bin.
10.	a	People leave the vehicle first; then you step on.
11.	c	Offer your seat to an elder, a pregnant or disabled person, etc.
12.	c	The trip was exciting for you but don't bore or overwhelm others.

Event	Answer	CONDOLENCE - Correct Responses with Rationale
1.	b	Help by bringing a meal, babysitting for young children, or just listening.
2.	b	Be respectful at the service. Do not chat or gossip.
3.	a	Share your condolences with the family, even if you do not know them.
4.	a	The funeral is not a style show nor is it a place for jeans.
5.	b	The family will appreciate hearing a nice story about their loved one.
6.	b	We never know how someone else feels, nor do we know if it's for the best.
7.	c	This isn't the time to speculate or to ask family.
8.	b	Briefly, say "My name is Jane Doe and I know John from work."
9.	c	A good friend is one who is willing to listen.
10.	a	Tell the family you are sorry for their loss before you spend time with anyone else.
11.	b	Most important is a card with your condolences or a phone call if you know them well.
12.	c	This is a time to be respectful of people who are grieving.

Consider Consideration

Open this for older or disabled people.	What is *a door*
Cover your nose and mouth with this when you cough or sneeze.	What is *a tissue or into your elbow*
Do this for a person in a wheelchair or a ride-on scooter in a grocery store.	What is *retrieve an item from a high shelf*
Don't do this with a cashier when people are lined up behind you.	What is *chat*
Don't do this at a movie.	What is *talk*
Do this when you walk your dog.	What is *clean up after your dog*
Never park here unless you officially need it.	What is *the handicapped parking spot*
Never do this when someone is waiting for a parking place.	What is *sneak in*
Do this after putting shopping bags in your car.	What is *return the shopping cart*
Do this after using the bathroom.	What is *clean up after yourself*
Do not do this if you eat out with someone who is older than you.	What is *assume they will pay*
Do not do this if you see someone who looks different from you.	What is *laugh, stare or point*
When driving, do not do this except in an emergency.	What is *honk*
Do this for a needy neighbor.	What is *visit and help*
Do this before you offer a ride to a child.	What is *ask parental permission*
Do this to the volume of music in headphones in an indoor public place.	What *is keep it low*
Do this when you are attending a class.	What is *be on time*
Do this when someone achieves something.	What is *compliment or congratulate*
Do this if you have made a mistake.	What is *apologize and take responsibility*
Avoid asking about this topic.	What is *money, weight, age with older people, personal or family problems*

Consider Consideration

FOR THE FACILITATOR

I. Purpose

To consider and accommodate people's feelings and needs through everyday actions.

II. General Comments

This game reinforces that kindness and diplomacy improve others' lives and enhance teens' social skills.

III. Possible Activities

a. Before session photocopy and cut the *Consider Consideration* handout on the broken lines.

b. Place cutouts face down on table in front of the room.

c. Before session coach two volunteers to portray this pantomime:
One carries a pile of books in arms and struggles to open the door; the other stands back and watches.

d. Ask audience to identify the problem in the scenario (the other person needs to open the door).

e. Write *What is Consideration?* on the board and ask its definition (thoughtfulness, concern).

f. Explain that teens will take turns picking up a clue and reading aloud.

g. Peers will guess the correct response which must start with *What is*; after one responds, teens call out others' possible ideas.

h. Remind teens to read aloud only the bold text sentence on the left side of the cutout; the suggested response is on the right in regular text.

i. Read aloud this example:
Use this word when you ask for something (elicit the response – *What is please*).

j. Teens take turns reading a clue; the first to say *What is* ... with the correct response earns a turn.

k. Teens who blurt out an answer without *What is* ... do not earn the next turn (this adds challenge to the game).

l. If a teen who already had a turn responds correctly, a teen who has not had a chance takes the next turn to pick up and read a clue aloud.

IV. Enrichment Activities

a. Ask for clarification regarding a couple of the game clues:
   - Why cough or sneeze into your tissue or the inside of your elbow and not into your hand? (Your hands touch things and/or people and spread germs).
   - Why ask parental or caregiver permission before giving a ride to a child? (They may want the child to walk or may want the child transported only by family members or adults).

b. Ask teens to brainstorm their *pet peeves* of people's inconsiderate actions and ways to rectify them; a volunteer lists their ideas on the board.

c. Encourage teens to compose their own clues (to be written on slips of paper, picked up by peers and read aloud as in the above game, or to state aloud clues for peers to respond to).

Win at Work

Each team lists their ideas in the applicable section below.

TEAM: Interviews	**TEAM: Cooperation with Co-Workers**
1. ____________	1. ____________
2. ____________	2. ____________
3. ____________	3. ____________
4. ____________	4. ____________
5. ____________	5. ____________
6. ____________	6. ____________
7. ____________	7. ____________
8. ____________	8. ____________
9. ____________	9. ____________
10. ____________	10. ____________
TEAM: Accepting Supervision	**TEAM: Work Habits**
1. ____________	1. ____________
2. ____________	2. ____________
3. ____________	3. ____________
4. ____________	4. ____________
5. ____________	5. ____________
6. ____________	6. ____________
7. ____________	7. ____________
8. ____________	8. ____________
9. ____________	9. ____________
10. ____________	10. ____________

Win at Work

FOR THE FACILITATOR

I. Purpose

To heighten awareness of social expectations in the workplace.
To be successful in the working world.

II. General Comments

Teens practice teamwork as they brainstorm employment-related concepts.

III. Possible Activities

Ask teens to discuss ways to get and keep a job (accept any reasonable responses).
Distribute the *Win at Work* handout and ask teens to pick the team topic that interests them most.
Encourage a fairly even distribution of teens per team; teammates sit near each other in four clusters. (Facilitator circulates among teams giving hints and reinforcing their work).
Teammates brainstorm ten concepts (or more) for their topic only; a writer for each team notes their ideas on their team's section of the handout.
Teens re-convene; writers or teams take turns sharing their lists of ideas; peers provide feedback.

Examples

TEAM: Interviews
1. Good grooming and hygiene; proper dress
2. Turn cell phone OFF
3. Good eye contact
4. Smile
5. Firm handshake
6. Research in advance the company and job
7. Ask work-related questions (not about pay or benefits)
8. Prepare to highlight strengths
9. Put weaknesses in a positive light, i.e., if experience is limited, stress being a quick learner
10. Say *Thank you* and send a thank you note

TEAM: Cooperation with Co-Workers
1. Listen and learn
2. Do not gossip
3. Help others
4. Refill and replace items as you use them
5. If issues arise, talk to the person first versus going over someone's head to the boss
6. Don't try to sell things to co-workers
7. Do not interrupt conversations
8. Respect closed doors; knock if necessary to see the person inside; ask if it is okay to enter a workspace or office or cubicle
9. Keep voice volume low
10. Leave a note or return later if someone is on a phone call; don't eavesdrop.

TEAM: Accepting Supervision
1. Listen to and repeat instructions
2. Ask questions for clarification
3. Accept constructive criticism
4. Ask about ways to improve
5. Try to resolve conflict with supervisor versus going over the person's head
6. Do not *bad mouth* the boss
7. If you share a complaint, suggest a solution
8. Make your interactions quick and focused
9. Acknowledge your mistakes and apologize
10. Respect the voice of reason and experience

TEAM: Work Habits
1. Be on time
2. Maintain good attendance
3. Focus on quality and quantity
4. Use cell phone during breaks only
5. No personal use of the work computers
6. Be pleasant to customers (even rude ones)
7. Upgrade skills through education
8. Call as soon as possible if unable to work
9. Avoid slang, profanity, off-color, sexist, racist, or ethnic jokes or remarks
10. Give a two-week notice before quitting

IV. Enrichment Activities

Encourage teens to discuss other work-related issues. Examples: to use a chain of command and/or Human Resources if an issue cannot be worked out with a supervisor; to assertively say *No* to unwanted overtime work; to politely decline an assignment for which one has not been trained; to never steal money, supplies or others' ideas; to give credit to co-workers when warranted, etc.

Sportsmanship Pyramid

Game Show Host Instructions

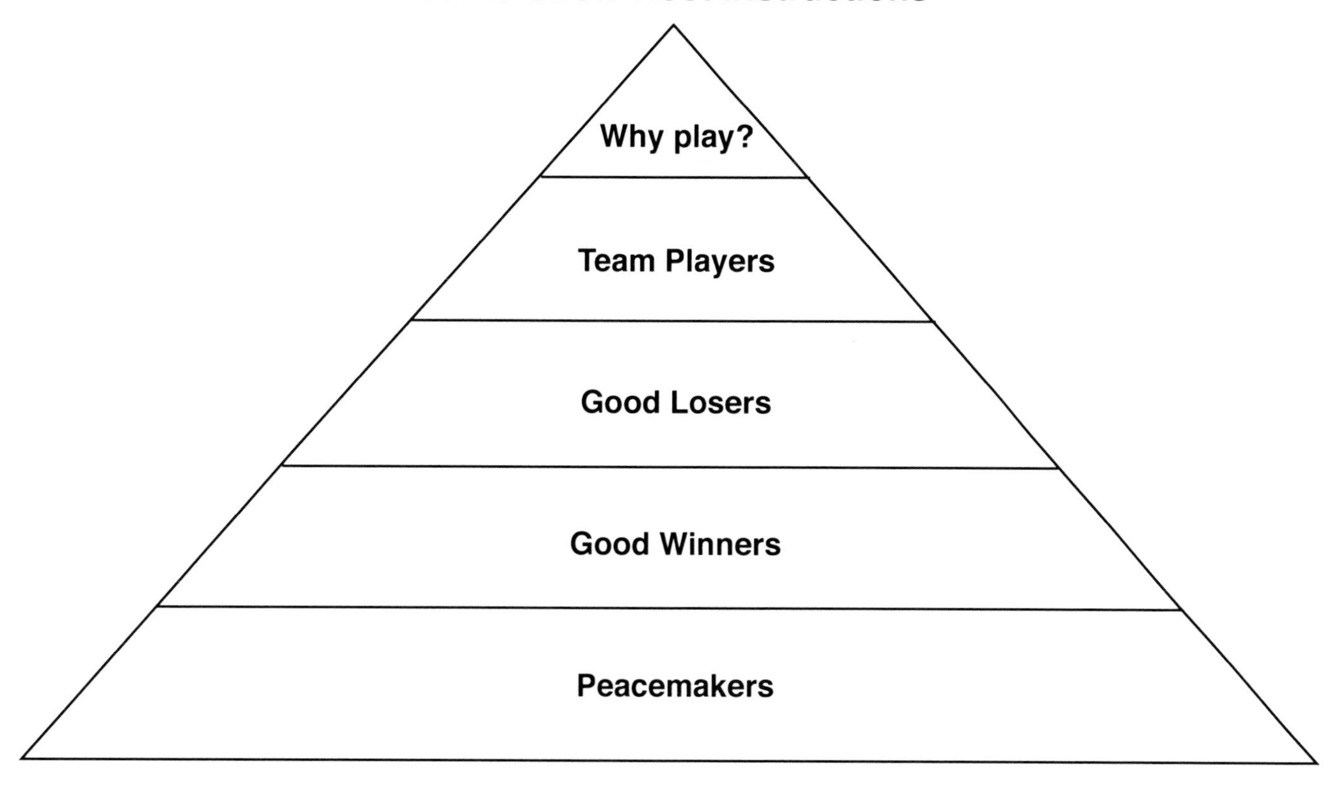

Copy the pyramid and words onto the board. Divide the group into two teams. Ask a scorekeeper to write each team's points on the board and to call "time's up" after thirty seconds.

Read the following to the players before the game starts:

1. When a team chooses a category, I will read a hint and allow thirty seconds for the right response.
2. If one team does not guess the exact word or phrase, the other team has thirty seconds to try.
3. If neither team guesses correctly I will reveal the answer.
4. Each correct response earns a point; the team with the most points wins the game.

Host please note: Hints are in regular text. Answers are parenthesized and italicized.

Why Play?	Team Players	Good Losers	Good Winners	Peacemakers
For enjoyment *(fun)*	Play by the laws *(rules)*	Do this if you make an error *(admit it)*	Don't do this *(brag)*	Boxers touch each others' … *(gloves)*
To move around *(exercise)*	Give this when someone makes a good play *(credit)*	Show this regarding official decisions *(respect)*	Give this to opponents who did their best *(recognition)*	Opponents do this after a game *(shake hands)*
Teammates may become these *(friends)*	Show up for every training session *(practice)*	Do this to the winning team *(congratulate)*	Give this to teammates who helped win *(compliment)*	Never do this with the other team *(fight)*

Sportsmanship Pyramid

FOR THE FACILITATOR

Purpose

To reinforce good sportsmanship.

General Comments

Fair play is needed on the playing field and in life.

Possible Activities

a. Have a stop watch, hourglass or clock with a second hand available.
b. Explain that teens will play a game involving hints about words.
c. Teammates will work together to guess the exact word or phrase.
d. Give the *Sportsmanship Pyramid* handout to a volunteer host who follows the instructions.
e. Note that teammates confer and yell out their guesses for thirty seconds.
f. They must guess the exact word (italicized and parenthesized on the host's instructions).
g. After the game ask teens to demonstrate sportsmanship (shake hands with opponents, etc.).
h. Ask teens to share examples of good and bad sportsmanship they have observed.
i. Ask if teens would applaud good plays by opponents; why or why not?
j. Ask if teens would help an injured opponent off the field; why or why not?
k. Encourage teens to discuss ways to handle people who pressure them to win at all costs.
   Possibilities
   - State they are doing their best.
   - Be open to suggestions for improvement.
   - Explain they play to enjoy the sport.
l. Ask teens what they can do if people try to provoke a fight about a game (walk away, remember that violence is not sportsman-like and it is penalized, tell the coach, etc.)
m. Ask teens to brainstorm examples of *teams* in life; a peer lists their ideas on the board.
   Possibilities
   - A family
   - A group of co-workers
   - Performers in a band
   - Classmates who work together on a project
   - A choir, orchestra, drama club, debate team, etc.
   - Volunteers who work for a common cause
   - Members of a youth group

Enrichment Activities

a. Encourage teens to discuss their considerations when choosing a sport (for the love of the game and/or because the requirements align with their body builds and abilities).
b. Discuss options to join other teams like an academic decathlon for scholastic achievers, or a choir, drama club, band or orchestra for musicians or actors.
c. Discuss that many people participate in activities knowing they probably won't be the best.
d. Ask teens about the kinds of teams they want to join.
   Possibilities
   - Teammates respect each other, opponents and officials.
   - Every member has the chance to play, not just those with the most talent.
   - Playing your best matters more than winning.
   - Losses are viewed as learning experiences.
   - The team takes responsibility for losses rather than blaming a player.
   - The team shares the glory of winning rather than singling out a star.

FITTING IN 3

After the game, the king and the pawn go into the same box.

~ Italian Proverb

Parent / Caregiver Puzzle

Some teens feel as if they don't fit in at home.

Write the letters (below) that describe your parents / caregivers on the puzzle pieces.

a. They suffered childhood neglect and/or abuse.
b. They are in an unstable partner or marital relationship.
c. They have addictions.
d. They experience emotional problems.

If any of the above do not apply to you, write whatever you would like on the blank puzzle pieces.

WORD BANK

problems	feelings	peers	self-esteem	fault

Use the above word bank to complete the following sentences:

1. If I feel left out at home it's not my ____________________.
2. My parents or caregivers did their best but may have had their ____________________.
3. I can develop relationships with ____________________.
4. I can learn to express ____________________.
5. I can raise my ____________________.

Parent/Caregiver Puzzle

FOR THE FACILITATOR

I. Purpose

To recognize that parents/caregivers may have issues that affect their ability to nurture.

II. General Comments

Teens with problems at home may experience impaired social development and rejection by peers.

Parents/caregivers are not blamed but teens are helped to find ways to understand and overcome dysfunction.

III. Possible Activities

a. Before session coach two volunteers to perform this skit:
- A caregiver is reading when a child enters the room. The child cries, *They were mean to me at school!*
- The caregiver says *I'm busy. Leave me alone. It was probably all your fault anyway.*
- Performers take their seats.

b. Ask audience how they think the child felt (rejected, unimportant, deserving of mistreatment).

c. Ask teens to brainstorm caregiver factors that lead to unkindness, neglect and/or abuse; a peer lists ideas on board.

Possibly caregiver ...
- was not nurtured in childhood.
- doesn't recognize or express emotions.
- is in an unstable relationship.
- receives no support from friends or family.
- experiences stressful circumstances, like poverty.
- lacks knowledge about parenting.

d. Ask teens to brainstorm possible effects of parental rejection on children; a peer lists ideas on board.

Possible effects
- Sensitive to rejection at school
- Choice of inappropriate friends
- Learning problems
- Difficulty managing emotions
- Limited compassion for others
- Risky behaviors

e. Distribute the *Parental/Caregiver Puzzle* handout and allow time for completion.

f. Answers: 1. fault; 2. problems; 3. peers; 4. feelings; 5. self-esteem

g. Encourage teens to share their responses

IV. Enrichment Activities

a. Encourage a discussion of behaviors developed in neglectful home life that might lead to a child or teen being rejected by peers (passive and /or isolative, attention-seeking, disruptive, etc.).

b. Encourage a discussion regarding solutions: tutoring for learning problems; support system outside the family like mentoring programs, scouting, sports, etc.; therapy for teens; family therapy and social services to help with employment, housing, nutrition and other needs; spiritual sources of support like youth groups or religious institutions.

Dr. Fell's Press Conference

Announcer: Ladies and gentlemen, may I introduce the famous Dr. Fell and Mr. Brown.

Dr. Fell: I wish to read a disturbing letter I received from Mr. Tom Brown. It says:

I do not love thee, Dr. Fell
The reason why I cannot tell;
But this I know, and know full well,
I do not love thee Dr. Fell.
~Tom Brown

1st Reporter: Dr. Fell, how does it feel to be so disliked?

Dr. Fell: Terrible.

2nd Reporter: Mr. Brown, why do you dislike Dr. Fell?

Mr. Brown: I do not know.

3rd Reporter: Dr. Fell, can you make this man like you?

Dr. Fell: No. I've tried everything. Nothing works.

Consider the poem and complete the sentences:

Explain why it is or is not realistic to expect everyone to like you.

____

Explain why it is or is not realistic to wonder why someone dislikes you.

____

Explain why it is or is not realistic to feel upset every time someone rejects you.

____

Name inappropriate things you have done to try to make people like you.

____

____

____

What was a time you disliked someone for no known reason?

____

____

____

Dr. Fell's Press Conference

FOR THE FACILITATOR

I. Purpose

To recognize the futility of seeking affection and/or approval from everyone.

II. General Comments

Teens often pursue popularity at all costs; teens often feel devastated when not accepted.

III. Possible Activities

a. Before session coach six teens to play: Announcer, Dr. Fell, Mr. Brown, first, second & third reporters.
b. Distribute the *Dr. Fell's Press Conference* handout to the actors only.
c. Allow a few minutes for actors to select and rehearse their roles before the presentation.
d. Actors need not memorize their lines and may read from scripts as they perform.
e. When session starts Announcer, Dr. Fell and Mr. Brown stand in front of the room.
f. Reporters sit in the first row of audience seats.
g. Advise audience they will see a mock press conference.
h. The press conference is portrayed.
i. Actors return to their seats.
j. Ask audience for their impressions of the skit (responses will vary).
k. Distribute the *Dr. Fell's Press Conference* handout to the audience teens.
l. Allow time for the actors and audience to complete the handout.
m. Encourage teens to share their responses.

Possibilities

- Explain why it is or is not realistic to expect everyone to like you.
  Not realistic; they won't.
- Explain why it is or is not realistic to wonder why someone dislikes you.
  Not realistic; there may be no reason.
- Explain why it is or is not realistic to feel upset every time someone rejects you?
  Not realistic; you'll be upset most of the time.
- Name inappropriate things you have done to make people like you.
  Act phony, engage in risky behaviors, go along with the crowd against my better judgment, keep quiet when I wish I had spoken up, fail to right a wrong due to fear of criticism, etc.
- What was a time you disliked someone for no known reason?
  Answers will vary.

n. Encourage teens to discuss whether the poem justifies being unkind or rude (no; people who treat others with respect need not wonder about what they did to cause a negative reaction).

IV. Enrichment Activities

a. Encourage teens to brainstorm the effects of people-pleasing (trying to gain everyone's approval).
b. A peer lists their ideas.

Possibilities

- Hold in feelings like anger or sadness; eventual explosiveness, resentment, depression.
- Inability to say *No* or to voice opinions that are different; to lose one's identity.
- May enter relationships with someone who wants to influence them in an unhealthy way.
- Might do things they do not want to do even though they know better.

c. Encourage a discussion of what people-pleasers are seeking (acceptance, love, attention, friendship).
d. Ask teens to identify what a perpetual people-pleaser might do to break the cycle (admit it; express needs and opinions; say *no*; understand that respectful disagreement or confrontation can be productive; know that self-love and self-acceptance are the priorities and realize they will attract some people who do accept them for their genuine identities.)

New on the Block

1. Share a time when **you were new** in a neighborhood, a school or in a work or volunteer setting.

___

2. How did you feel when **you were new**?

___

3. **Accept**: When you see a new person, especially if they are different on the outside (appearance, accent, disability, etc.) what do you think they are feeling inside? Write your response in the thought bubble.

4. **Acknowledge**: What can you say to show you notice the person?

5. **Ask**: What open-ended question can you ask?

6. **Help**: What can you do to help the new person feel comfortable?

In a class ___

At lunch ___

At a job or volunteer site ___

In your neighborhood___

In an organization or activity ___

New on the Block

FOR THE FACILITATOR

I. Purpose

To have empathy and welcome newcomers or potential outsiders.

II. General Comments

Teens may be reluctant to accept new people, especially if the new people seem different. Teens will identify a new person's probable feelings and needs, and plan ways to include rather than exclude.

III. Possible Activities

a. Write on the board *New on the Block* and ask what comes to mind (being new in a neighborhood, class or elsewhere; teens may mention a musical group).

b. Ask teens to identify hurtful and helpful examples of how a new person reacts:
   - Thoughts (Examples – *I'll never make it here* versus *I'll give it a chance*).
   - Feelings (Examples – hopeless versus hopeful).
   - Actions (Examples – isolate self from people versus speak to people).

c. Distribute the *New on the Block* handout and allow time for completion.

d. Encourage teens to share their responses. Possibilities correspond to numbers on the handout.
   1. Answers will vary based on experiences.
   2. Feelings might be fear of the unknown, anxiety, loneliness, feeling like an outsider, etc.
   3. Acceptance thoughts might be *The person's feelings are a lot like mine.* or *The person may feel uncomfortable and want to be included.*
   4. Acknowledgement might be *I think you are new?* or I don't think I've seen you here before.
   5. An open-ended question might be "What was your old school like?" or *How does this compare to your other school, job, volunteer setting, team?*
   6. Help the new person to feel comfortable:
      - ✔ Tell the student something about the teacher or assignments; offer a copy of recent notes to help the person catch up.
      - ✔ Invite the newcomer to sit with you at lunch; introduce the person to your friends.
      - ✔ Show the worker easier ways to do the tasks; introduce the person to co-workers.
      - ✔ Inform the neighbor about local restaurants and recreation; introduce the person to people who live nearby.
      - ✔ Explain about the organization's history or share your feelings about the activity.

IV. Enrichment Activities

Encourage teens to role play scenarios (school, work, etc.) to show acceptance of newcomers.
Encourage teens to brainstorm other questions they might ask a new person.

Possibilities

- School (ask about subjects the new person likes and dislikes)
- Accomplishments (if the person was on any type of a team, ask about prior team performance)
- Abilities (if the newcomer seems to have special skills, ask how the person developed them)
- Activities (ask about the newcomer's favorite interests or favorite activities for free time)
- Change (ask what was easy and difficult about switching schools, jobs or moving, etc.)
- Arts (ask about the new person's favorite musical group, song, book, movie, artwork, etc.)
- Goals (ask about the newcomer's hopes regarding the new situation.)

Personality by the Numbers

Social Cues

1. You receive a high grade on a test; your friend looks upset when receiving test results.
   a. You share your joy with your friend.
   b. You ask your friend *What mark did you get?*
   c. You say nothing.
2. Your class learns about proper nutrition and exercise today. Your friend has a weight issue.
   a. You tactfully suggest that your friend focus on health.
   b. You ask your friend's opinion about the class topic.
   c. You talk about your own food and activity patterns.
3. You overhear your two cousins argue; one is crying.
   a. You ask the crying cousin *What seems to be the problem?*
   b. You go ask the other cousin *What did you do to cause the tears?*
   c. You ask both *Would it help to take a break to cool down?*

Team Player

4. You and peers complete a science project and win; you did most of the work.
   a. You give equal credit to your peers.
   b. You remind them you did most of the work.
   c. You tell everyone the project won because of your hard work.
5. You try out for a team and are not chosen.
   a. You claim there was favoritism.
   b. You go to the games and cheer for your team.
   c. You boycott the games.
6. You are on a clean-up crew and were given a task everyone else refused.
   a. You do the work.
   b. You complain.
   c. You ask someone to switch with you.

Self Control

7. You act friendly to someone and are treated coldly.
   a. You tell the person off.
   b. You take time to think about it.
   c. You tell other people about it.
8. You have a crush on a person who just asked your best friend out.
   a. You tell your friend you hope they have fun.
   b. You pressure your friend to cancel the date.
   c. You tell the person something unkind about your best friend.
9. Someone dents your car.
   a. You yell *You should've been more careful.*
   b. You tell police the driver was probably texting (although you did not witness it).
   c. You exchange insurance information and accept the driver's apology.

Empathy

10. Your friend's partner ends their relationship. Your friend is devastated. You say:
    a. *You'll find somebody else before you know it.*
    b. *It really must hurt.*
    c. *You two were never really compatible.*

(Continued on page 63)

Personality by the Numbers

FOR THE FACILITATOR

I. Purpose

To incorporate positive attributes into personality and behavior.

II. General Comments

This game addresses personality traits that aid social competence.

III. Possible Activities

a. Before session photocopy the list of questions 1-21, pages 61 and 65, for the game show host and the back of the second page of questions (Answer Key, and the Trait Number cutouts, page 64).
b. Cut the Answer Key and Trait Number cutouts on the broken lines.
c. Cutouts show the corresponding trait (instead of numbers only) so teens focus on the qualities.
d. Shuffle the cutouts and place in a stack.
e. When session begins list terms on the board; ask how they contribute to a pleasant personality.
Possibilities
- Social Cues – awareness of others' emotions helps teens interact appropriately.
- Team Player – cooperation rather than wanting all the control or credit wins friends.
- Self Control – to suppress angry, jealous or impulsive reactions and substitute kindness is appealing.
- Empathy – to put one's self in another's place is a key to sensitive responses.
- Flexibility – teens who roll with the punches are easy to be around.
- Influence – teens can empower themselves to improve their social environments.
- Helpfulness –teens who aid others enhance their sense of purpose and usually are appreciated.

f. Give the *Personality by the Numbers* handout to a game show host who sits at front of the room.
g. Give the Answer Key to the game show host.
h. Distribute the stack of Trait Number cutouts to peers; each takes the top one and passes the stack.
i. If more than twenty-one peers are present, teens with no cutout will identify a positive personality trait and state one way to demonstrate it. Example: Kindness – Give a compliment.
j. Teens take turns revealing their Trait Number cutouts; host asks the corresponding questions.
k. Teens may request peer assistance as needed.
l. Teens share reasons for their response; then game show host may read the rationale.
m. The rationales provided are examples only; teens may have other excellent reasons for responses.

IV. Enrichment Activities

Ask teens to brainstorm traits they do and don't want in a friend. A peer lists their ideas.
Examples

Traits of a True Friend	Negative Behaviors
Helps me achieve goals	Undermines my goals or achievements
Helps me feel good about myself	Puts me down
Trustworthy	Disloyal
Can laugh at self	Laughs at me or others
Listens	Talks too much
Similar values	Different values
Willing to try new (safe, appropriate) things	Rigid *stick in the mud*
Cooperative	Bossy
Expects to give and take	*My way or the highway*

Personality by the Numbers

Empathy *(continued)*

11. A family crisis occurs. You tell your relatives:
    a. *Someday we'll be able to laugh about it.*
    b. *We'll help each other through it.*
    c. *A lot of families have worse problems.*
12. A friend is upset because parents/caregivers are splitting up. You say:
    a. *"This will probably disrupt your life, won't it?*
    b. *It's best to separate if they can't get along.*
    c. *Let's go to a movie to get your mind off of it.*

Flexibility

13. You go to a party; it is outdoors and you hate flies.
    a. You inform people that flies carry germs.
    b. You cover your food and eat it before the flies do.
    c. You offer to shoo flies away while others eat.
14. You usually work the cash register; your boss asks you to cut vegetables instead.
    a. You say *It's not in my job description.*
    b. You accept the assignment willingly.
    c. You cut vegetables but give people the silent treatment.
15. After a hectic day you go to a take-out restaurant. They run out of the food you crave.
    a. You yell at the worker.
    b. You tell the manager you'll call corporate headquarters about their poor planning.
    c. You choose an alternative meal.

Influence

16. Students are disgruntled about a situation at school.
    a. You tell them *It is what it is.*
    b. You bring up more evidence to heat things up.
    c. You suggest drafting a respectful petition together.
17. Your friend bullies someone.
    a. You ask your friend to stop.
    b. You go with the flow.
    c. You walk away.
18. Your school has no activities related to your particular passion.
    a. You decide to forget about it.
    b. You write a letter to the superintendant requesting a new club.
    c. You find like-minded peers to go with you to the principal.

Helpfulness

19. Your classmate struggles with a subject that is easy for you.
    a. You let the person see your finished homework.
    b. You offer to help the person study.
    c. You suggest a tutor.
20. Your relative is diagnosed with a serious illness.
    a. You reassure the person that medical science will find a cure.
    b. You give the person several articles about the condition.
    c. You offer to go to a support group with the relative.
21. Your friend shares a secret about being abused.
    a. You honor your friend's request for secrecy.
    b. You provide a shoulder to cry on.
    c. You offer to go with your friend to tell authorities or a trusted adult.

Personality by the Numbers

Answer Key

1. c. Do not brag or ask about a mark; your friend's face shows disappointment.
2. b. Ask an open-ended question; your friend might share concern about health.
3. c. Make a helpful suggestion; neither interrogate nor assume one caused the tears.
4. a. Generosity means to share the glory; otherwise you take credit but lose respect.
5. b. Cheer for your team; you lose a spot on the team but gain a reputation for team spirit.
6. a. Sometimes *Just do it*; if you are repeatedly given the worst assignment, then speak-up.
7. b. Take time to think; you can't control someone's actions but can control your reactions.
8. a. Sometimes you have to accept disappointment and wish others the best.
9. c. To yell or accuse does not reverse the damage to your car; don't damage your behavior.
10. b. Show empathy for pain; trying to cheer someone up trivializes the emotions and situation.
11. b. Emphasize mutual support; do not minimize the crisis.
12. a. Encourage friend to elaborate on how the split-up affects his/her life.
13. b. Discretely protect yourself but don't insult the host by mentioning the flies.
14. b. You may win points with the boss and peers to do duties as assigned.
15. c. You understand that this can happen; if the problem recurs often, then talk politely to manager.
16. c. You will be part of the solution rather than giving up or adding fuel to the flame.
17. a. Speak up to stop the bully; if the bully des not listen to you, privately tell authorities.
18. c. Show leadership by recruiting others for your cause; (a joint letter might be done later).
19. b. Helpfulness is an attractive trait; if you do not have time or skills, you might suggest a tutor.
20. c. Emotional support is needed first; information later; too many facts overwhelm at this stage.
21. c. Your friend may need your moral support to reveal the abuse.

Cut on the dotted line above and give Answer Key to game show host.
Cut-out the Trait Number boxes below, shuffle and place in a stack for peers.

Trait Numbers

Social Cues 1	**Social Cues 2**	**Social Cues 3**	**Team Player 4**	**Team Player 5**	**Team Player 6**	**Self Control 7**
Self Control 8	**Self Control 9**	**Empathy 10**	**Empathy 11**	**Empathy 12**	**Flexibility 13**	**Flexibility 14**
Flexibility 15	**Influence 16**	**Influence 17**	**Influence 18**	**Helpfulness 19**	**Helpfulness 20**	**Helpfulness 21**

End Exclusion and Embrace Inclusion Acrostic

Exclusion means to keep out. Inclusion welcomes differences in diverse groups. Think about words and phrases that relate to these concepts. Write them next to the letters.

Example: **E**mpathy *(have empathy and consider how it feels to be excluded.)*

E ______________________________

X ______________________________

C ______________________________

L ______________________________

U ______________________________

S ______________________________

I ______________________________

O ______________________________

N ______________________________

I ______________________________

N ______________________________

C ______________________________

L ______________________________

U ______________________________

S ______________________________

I ______________________________

O ______________________________

N ______________________________

End Exclusion and Embrace Inclusion Acrostic

FOR THE FACILITATOR

I. Purpose

To avoid negative stereotyping, celebrate individuality, show empathy for perceived outsiders.

II. General Comments

Teens may be wary of people who are different and may fear being perceived as different from peers.

III. Possible Activities

a. Write *Exclusion* on the board and ask its meaning (to keep out).
b. Write *Empathy* on the board and ask its meaning (to understand another person's feelings).
c. Ask teens to share reasons people are kept out of peer groups (because they are different, etc.).
d. Elicit reasons teens may avoid people who seem different (fear of the unknown, unsure how to treat a person with a disability, worried they might not understand an accent, etc.).
e. Ask teens if most of their friends are similar to themselves or different and why; answers will vary.
f. Write *Inclusion* on the board and ask its meaning (the presence of somebody in a group).
g. Ask teens the advantages of being friends with a variety people (learn about different cultures, etc.).
h. Distribute the *End Exclusion and Embrace Inclusion Acrostic* handout to teams or individuals.
i. Teens may find the activity more meaningful if they brainstorm with teammates.
j. Allow time for completion.
k. Encourage individuals or team leaders to share their responses.
l. Read aloud the words for each letter below and elicit from teens the parenthesized explanations:

Expand (expand ideas by mingling with people from different backgrounds)
X-Out (x-out or cross out discrimination and prejudice)
Contact (contact breaks down barriers between people from different groups)
Look (look for individual traits rather than assuming typical characteristics among group members)
Universality (we're all members of the human race with more similarities than differences)
Stop (stop stereotyping, stop people from excluding peers)
Include (involve rather than ban people)
One (one person can make a difference by encouraging peers to accept rather than reject someone)
Never (never believe that all members of a group have the same characteristics)

Information (ask about a person's culture, beliefs, likes and dislikes)
Negate stereotypes (look for distinctive traits within each person)
Celebrate differences (one's own and others')
Learn (to value various perspectives)
Understand (that it hurts to be left out)
Speak up (advocate against bigotry to improve and possibly save lives)
Insight (recognize and refute negative labels about one's own culture)
Open-mindedness (respect people's rights even if opinions differ)
Notice (spot someone who is being ignored and involve the person in an activity)

IV. Enrichment Activities

If teens are willing, encourage volunteers to share …

- Times they were not accepted due to being seen as different.
- Times they were included in a group despite differences.
- Times they got to know someone and realized the person was more like them than different.

Pieces of Shy

Host reads directions to the group:

"When it is your turn, come to the front of the room and read a statement from this master copy. Everyone please listen carefully to each piece of information. There will be a quiz."

1. Shyness is discomfort around people and fear of their negative reactions.
2. Technology has decreased face-to-face contact.
3. Shy behavior includes speech at a low volume.
4. Shy behavior may include avoidance of eye contact.
5. Physical symptoms may include increased heart rate, dry mouth and shaking.
6. People with shyness symptoms may feel faint, dizzy, or as if they have butterflies in their stomachs.
7. Cognitive symptoms relate to thoughts about self, others and the situation.
8. Negative thoughts like *I'm helpless and others have power* may lead to shy behavior.
9. Emotional symptoms may include self-consciousness and low self-esteem.
10. People who experience shyness may feel lonely, depressed and anxious.
11. Some people who experience shyness are high achievers and are kind to others.
12. In some cultures shyness is considered respectful and thoughtful.
13. People who experience shyness tend to avoid new situations and contact with unknown people.
14. If people who feel shy force themselves to interact, the shyness may diminish.
15. Positive thoughts about self and others often decrease shyness.
16. People who learn and practice social skills gain confidence.
17. This exercise helps decrease shyness when speaking in front of a group.
18. This activity gives value to each person's piece of information.

✂- -

Self-Scored QUIZ

Write a letter on the line in front of each symptom. P - Physical, C - Cognitive, E - Emotional:

1. ______ Heart pounding, trembling, feeling like one might pass out
2. ______ Feelings of inadequacy
3. ______ Fear of unfamiliar people and places
4. ______ Thoughts like *I can't fit in.*

Write the letter T if the statement is true and F if the statement is false:

5. ______ It is best to avoid situations that might worsen shyness.
6. ______ Thoughts like *I can do this* help people face fears.
7. ______ Helping others takes a shy person's mind off self.
8. ______ Texting, Internet websites and e-mails prepare people well for face-to-face contact.

Complete the sentences below:

9. One common fear I faced during this activity was ______________________________

____

10. Listening to others during this activity helped me to ______________________________

____

✂- -

Pieces of Shy

FOR THE FACILITATOR

I. Purpose

To work together toward common knowledge and a common goal.

II. General Comments

The word *Quiz* and concepts of right and wrong answers are generally not used in this book. This session is an exception. This activity focuses on the **process** whereby teens share information that leads to a better outcome for all on the quiz. The content about shyness is secondary. The **actions** of speaking in front of a group, listening and valuing each person's piece of information are of primary importance. The quiz is self-scored and does not count for any grade. Teens who are extremely uncomfortable or unable to read aloud may decline; people with *slight* stage fright are encouraged to face their fears.

III. Possible Activities

a. Before session photocopy the *Pieces of Shy* handout, cut on the broken lines and reserve one copy of statements 1-18 (top portion of the handout); this is the master copy for the host.
b. Photocopy enough of the self-scored quiz (bottom portion of the handout) for each teen.
c. Explain that teens will teach each other some shyness concepts and then take a self-scored quiz.
d. A host will stay at the front of the room and cross off statements as they are read aloud by peers.
e. Provide the host with the master copy of the statements; retain copies of the quiz until later.
f. Host reads aloud the directions then calls on teens to come up to the front and read aloud a statement.
g. Host crosses off the statements as they are read; after eighteen turns distribute the quiz.
h. Allow a few minutes for teens to complete the quiz; then they self-score.

Answers

1. P
2. E
3. E
4. C
5. F
6. T
7. T
8. F
9. *Example*: Fear of public speaking, of being on stage or the center of attention.
10. *Example*: Learn information for the quiz but more importantly to value everyone's input.

IV. Enrichment Activities

a. Encourage teens to share their experiences with shyness.
b. Ask teens to brainstorm ways to overcome shyness; a peer lists ideas on the board.

Possibilities

- Use positive self-talk.
- Visualize yourself acting confident in a social situation.
- *Just do it!* Practice facing people and environments you previously avoided.
- Volunteer at charitable, social, political or spiritual organizations or for arts or cultural activities.
- Practice skills with friends or family. (How to introduce yourself, start and continue a conversation).
- Talk verbally on the cell phone and meet friends in person rather than depending on cyber-security.

Corner Shyness

Opener Corner Coach

Your job is to encourage peers to do the following:

- Smile.
- Make eye contact.
- Introduce themselves.
- Ask an open-ended question that requires elaboration.
- Listen to the response and then keep the conversation going.

Compliment Corner Coach

Your job is to encourage peers to do the following:

- Look person in the eye.
- Give a compliment.
- Receive a compliment graciously by saying *Thank You.*

Comment Corner Coach

Your job is to encourage peers to do the following:

- Make a comment about the current situation, school, class, etc.
- Ask an opinion about the same situation.
- Listen to the response and then keep the conversation going.
- Be confident

Clue Corner Coach

Your job is to encourage peers to do the following:

- Consider positive information or an observation about the person.
- Start a conversation about a topic of interest to the other person.
- *Example*: Use knowledge – *I know you're on the team. How did you get started in the sport?*
- *Example*: Make an observation – *I see you are in this class; what other classes do you take?*

Opener Corner	**Compliment Corner**	**Comment Corner**	**Clue Corner**

Corner Shyness

FOR THE FACILITATOR

I. Purpose

To coach peers, practice social skills and gain confidence.

II. General Comments

Teens face simulated situations and practice initiating and continuing face-to-face interactions.

III. Possible Activities

a. Before session photocopy the *Corner Shynes*s handout and cut on the broken lines.
b. Post the labels in the corners of the room (*Opener, Compliment, Comment, Clue Corner*).
c. Ask teens what a corner person does in boxing (observes the boxer, suggests strategies to win).
d. Ask four teens to volunteer to be Corner Coaches; they will help peers practice social skills.
e. Distribute one Corner Coach cut-out to each volunteer; coaches position themselves in corners.
f. Remaining peers partner with the person next to them and visit each corner consecutively.
g. Each corner coach tells teen pairs what to do according to the cutout instructions.
h. Corner coaches may switch places with teens who have rotated through the four corners; this enables coaches to practice skills and peers to take leadership roles as coaches.
i. The activity continues until all teens have visited the four corner stations.
j. Encourage a discussion regarding which practice was most difficult, the easiest, and why.
k. Ask teens the benefits of playing coach (takes mind off self; helps others and reduces own shyness).

IV. Enrichment Activities

a. Ask teens to identify other social skills to practice.
   Possibilities
   - Ask a person out on a date.
   - Ask a person parent/caregiver for a privilege or favor.
   - Ask for help.
   - Apologize.
   - Suggest an improvement at school, work or home.
   - Suggest going someplace together with a prospective friend.
b. Teens label corners, write instructions for coaches and take turns teaching and practicing the skills.

The World's Mosaic

A mosaic is an image created by assembling small pieces of glass, stone or any other items. The mosaic can symbolize a mix of any type of group.

Create a mosaic by drawing pictures and symbols related to many different cultures of people you know or those you have read about.

Consider …

- Countries
- Food
- Cars
- Sports and martial arts
- Music and dance
- Clothing
- Arts and crafts
- Landmarks
- Hair and appearance
- Jewelry and piercings
- Holidays
- Architecture

The World's Mosaic

FOR THE FACILITATOR

Purpose

To identify the effects of culture on self and others; to welcome multicultural contributions to society.

General Comments

Teens will use their own artifacts to create a group mosaic showing today's teen culture, then create individual mosaics about ethnic, religious, racial and/or social groups.

Possible Activities

a. Before session prepare a large table or floor space as a backdrop for teens' modern mosaic.
b. As admission into group or at start of session ask each teen to place a belonging on the table or floor; this may be a cell phone, iPod, jewelry, cell phone, page of homework, make up, book, pen, backpack, belt, or other object.
c. Encourage teens to arrange items in a design rather than a pile, thus to create a modern mosaic.
d. Write Artifact on the board and ask its meaning (object of cultural interest).
e. Refer to display of belongings and ask *If in five hundred years someone found these artifacts, what would they learn about teen culture in the 2000s?* (Answers will vary).
f. Write Mosaic on the board and ask its meaning (an image created by a variety of small pieces).
g. Ask what teens have created on the table or floor (a mosaic of their group's culture).
h. Allow teens to retrieve their belongings.
i. Write *My country is a multi-cultural mosaic* on the board and elicit that many races, ethnic, religious and social groups contribute to its design.
j. Ask teens to brainstorm representations of various cultures; a volunteer lists their ideas
   Possibilities
   - Images related to their own countries and cultures.
   - Indicators of their parents' and grandparents' countries and cultures.
   - Spiritual and/or religious symbols related to their own and others' beliefs.
   - Descriptions they read or heard about.
   - Depictions in movies, photos, or ads regarding different ethnic, racial and social groups.
k. Encourage teens to think about ways to represent their ideas visually with icons, drawings, signs, etc.
l. Distribute *The World's Mosaic* handout.
m. Ask teens to read aloud the statements, lists and directions at the top of the page.
n. Allow time for completion; remind teens that artistic skills are not required.
o. Encourage teens to share their mosaics and explain their symbols and drawings.

Enrichment Activities

a. Distribute another *The World's Mosaic* handout (page 71) to participants; ask them to create a collage of their own culture.
b. Write *Melting Pot* on the board and explain it is different from the mosaic concept. Explain that it was thought that people from different cultures would assimilate or become more similar to each other; in a melting pot all ingredients blend together.
c. Write *Salad Bowl* on the board and elicit how it differs from a melting pot (all ingredients maintain their separate identities, help to flavor each other as they share a common bond – the salad).
d. Encourage teens to debate whether a *Melting Pot* or *Salad Bowl* is a better description of America and to explain their reasons.
e. Teens' opinions may vary; current trends are toward the *Salad Bowl* where many individual parts make up the whole.
f. Encourage a discussion about the benefits of both: some assimilation like common adherence to laws and respect for human rights, plus celebration of differences in beliefs, the arts, spirituality, etc.

FRIENDSHIP 4

There will always be people who are for you and against you, and it's pointless wasting time trying to win over some of the people who are against you. Spend time with people who are for you. Those relationships are worth it.

~ Cathy Hopkins

"I've Got Your Back" Charades

Pat yourself on the back.

How can you give an emotional pat on the back to someone you care about?

Get back at someone

How can you resist the urge to get back at someone?

Turn your back on someone.

Share feelings about someone on whom you would never turn your back.

Back off.

How can you effectively tell someone to back off?

Get off my back.

In what situation would you like to get someone off your back?

Behind my back.

What do you regret doing behind someone's back?

Back-stab.

How have you "stabbed" someone in the back with words or deeds?

Back me up.

In what situation(s) do you need someone to back you up?

Take a back seat.

In what situation are you willing to take a back seat?

I've got your back.

How do you show you've got someone's back?

The straw that broke the camel's back

What was the final action that caused one of your relationships to end?

Backslide.

In what relationship do you fall back into a bad habit when you try to get along?

My back is against the wall.

Share a time you felt your back was against the wall in a relationship.

Flat on my back.

If someone close to you was flat on his/her back emotionally, how could you help?

I'm backed into a corner.

Share the situation and how you felt when you were backed into a corner.

Carry on your back.

Describe a person you would "carry on your back" and not feel burdened.

A back brace.

A back brace reduces pain and strain. How can you do this for someone close to you?

Back-up.

How can you provide back-up for someone close to you?

Someone has my back.

How do you know when someone has your back?

Back on your word.

Share about a time you went back on your word.

Tired of taking a back seat

In what situation are you tired of taking a back seat?

"I've Got Your Back" Charades

FOR THE FACILITATOR

I. Purpose

To apply *"I've got your back"* to providing positive support.
To resist peer pressure to *"have peoples' backs"* aggressively.

II. General Comments

Everyone needs a support system. Teens will identify ways to safely defend friends and family.

III. Possible Activities

a. Before session photocopy the *"I've Got Your Back" Charade*s handout and cut on the broken lines.

b. Place the cutouts face down in front of the room.

c. Write on the board *I've got your back* and ask its meaning (to be supportive).

d. Ask how it might apply to physical aggression (fist-fights, gang violence).

e. Encourage a discussion of what it means to *have someone's back in a healthy way.*
Possibilities
- Do not gossip about the person.
- Verbally defend the person unless it would put you in danger.
- Privately and tactfully give constructive feedback if needed.
- Keep the person's personal information private (unless the person reveals intention to harm self, others, or suffers abuse).
- Prioritize the person's safety (warn the person about dangerous people or activities to avoid; tell a trusted adult if the person reveals life threatening issues like suicidal plans, etc.).
- Help the person defend him/herself by encouraging assertiveness (not aggression) unless it would result in danger.
- If it is unwise for the person to stick-up for him/herself, anonymously tell a trusted adult about threats or bullying.

f. Explain that teens will play *charades* and/or a drawing illustrations game with phrases related to the word *back.*

g. Teens take turns coming to the front of the room, picking a cutout and portraying the bold text word or phrase using body language or drawn illustrations.

h. Peers guess the words or phrases; the teen who guesses correctly then responds to the question(s) or statements on the cutout. (Teens may ask peers for help as needed).

i. The teen who correctly guesses the word or phrase and/or responds to the question takes the next turn.

IV. Enrichment Activities

a. Ask teens to share experiences when they stood up for themselves when no one *had their back.*

b. Encourage a discussion about times they would not support a friend or family member. *Examples*: If asked to lie, cheat, steal, do something illegal or against one's value system.

A Frenemy

The word frenemy blends two words friend and enemy.
A frenemy is an enemy pretending to be a friend.

Frenemies have two sides of their personality. You may like one side and dislike the other.

Possible Traits of Friends, Enemies or Both

A. Long term buddy
B. Have had fun times together
C. Plans activities together
D. Bitterly competitive
E. Jealous
F. Cancels at the last minute
G. Supports successes
H. Stays close during tough times
I. Gives backhanded compliments (*That outfit is really slimming.*)
J. Sabotages (You plan to study; the person says *Why bother?)*
K. Resents your victories
L. Builds up confidence
M. Bad-mouths you and others
N. Mutual dependence
O. Mutual gain
P. Mutual mistrust

Choose one Frenemy – Use name code _______.
Place the letters of the traits on the Friend, Enemy, or both sides of the figure below.

FRIEND SIDE **ENEMY SIDE**

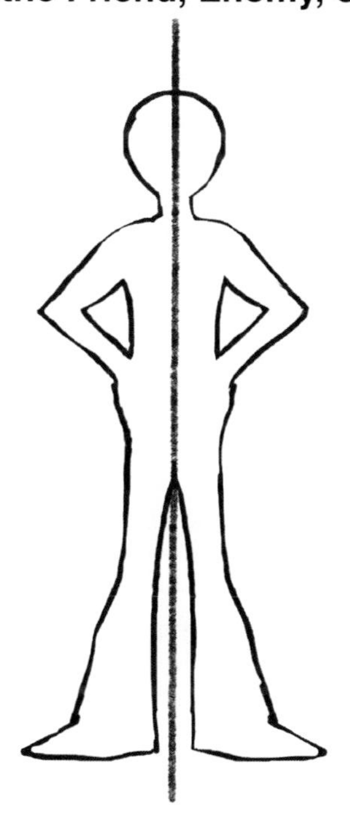

(Continued on page 79)

A Frenemy

FOR THE FACILITATOR

I. Purpose

To recognize the ambivalence caused by frenemy relationships and why teens stay in them. To use assertion to stop the negativity and to weigh whether to continue or to end the relationship.

II. General Comments

Often frenemies have been close for a long time and share memories and secrets. Because the relationship is both beneficial and detrimental, it is difficult to break away.

III. Possible Activities

a. Write *A Frenemy* on the board; ask teens its meaning (enemy posing as friend).
b. Ask teens if they remember the Disney movie *Frenemies* about the ups and downs of three pairs of friends.
c. Distribute one set of handouts to each participant, both pages 77 and 79, as each participant needs to be able to complete one for each frenemy.
d. Teens read aloud the introduction and instructions.
e. Ask teens to write about one person per set of handouts, who may be a frenemy, and respond about that person.
f. If participants have more than one frenemy, distribute additional sets of handouts for homework.
g. Allow time for completion; encourage teens to share their responses.

Possibilities with rationales

A. Long term buddy – May be both; the shared history makes it hard to end the relationship.
B. Have had fun times together – May be both; these memories keep them from splitting up.
C. Plans activities together – May be both; they may try to re-kindle the good times.
D. Bitterly competitive – Enemies; friends may compete but it can be vicious with enemies.
E. Jealous – Enemies are jealous; friends may envy but are not jealous.
F. Cancels at the last minute – Enemies cancel for a better offer; friends cancel in emergencies.
G. Supports successes – Friends; enemies downplay a victory or find fault.
H. Stays close during tough times – Both; enemies may stay close during trouble but are distant during triumphs due to jealousy.
I. Gives backhanded compliments – Enemies give a compliment with an intended unkind meaning.
J. Sabotages – Enemies.
K. Resents victories – Enemies.
L. Builds up confidence – Friends.
M. Bad-mouths you and others – Enemies.
N. Mutual dependence – May be both; with frenemies it's usually over-dependence.
O. Mutual gain – Friends; with enemies one's gain is another's loss due to *one-upmanship.*
P. Mutual mistrust – Enemies.

h. Ask teens to share their responses on the second page of the handout with the group and receive feedback.
i. Responses to questions and assertive sentence starters will vary.
j. If participants have more than one frenemy, distribute additional sets of handouts as homework.
k. Reinforce that it is easier to deal with a total enemy or true friend than a frenemy who has a combination of traits.

(See page 80 for enrichment activities.)

A Frenemy *(Continued)*

Add any additional friend and enemy traits you have noticed about the frenemy you listed on page 77.

____

____

____

____

How does this frenemy both help and hurt you?

Helps ____

____

____

____

Hurts ____

____

____

____

Discuss whether this frenemy-ship is worth it.

____

____

____

____

____

Plan how you can confront your frenemy's behavior:

I feel ______________________ when you ______________________

____

so ____

____

____

____

A Frenemy

FOR THE FACILITATOR *(Continued from page 76)*

IV. Enrichment Activities

a. Encourage teens to practice the assertive *I feel ... when you... so ...* during role plays related to their specific situations.

b. Encourage teens to weigh the pros and cons of continuing relationships with their frenemies.

c. Discuss whether teens might be more patient if the frenemies have backgrounds or problems that contribute to their negative behaviors; teens might suggest talking with a trusted adult.

d. Discuss whether frenemies can agree to disagree on certain topics or avoid certain situations (like not being around the other person's boy/girlfriend if they tend to flirt).

e. Ask teens when a clean break might be best (the cons heavily outweigh the pros; the teen feels seriously depressed, resentful, or gets lost in the frenemy's overbearing personality; the teen's hopes and dreams are degraded by the frenemy, etc.).

f. This concept can also be used in another session regarding family members.

Found Again

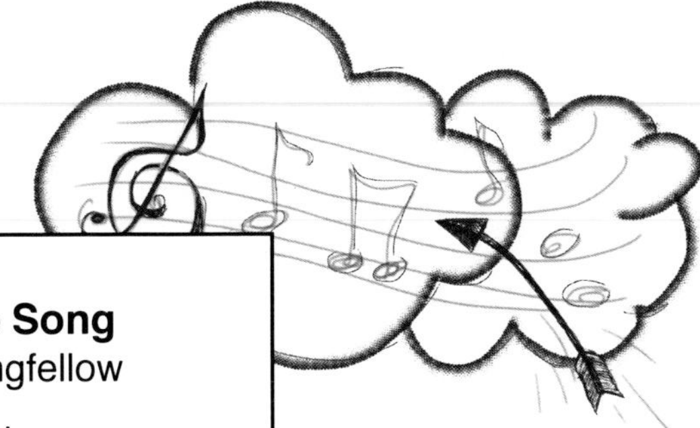

The Arrow and the Song
Henry Wadsworth Longfellow

I shot an arrow into the air,
It fell to earth, I knew not where;
For, so swiftly it flew, the sight
Could not follow in its flight.

I breathed a song into the air,
It fell to earth, I knew not where;
For who has sight so keen and strong,
That it can follow the flight of song?

Long, long afterward, in an oak
I found the arrow, still unbroke;
And the song, from beginning to end,
I found again in the heart of a friend.

1. Circle the two lines that mean most to you; explain why. ____________________

   ____

2. What was your arrow? ____________________

   ____

3. Where might it have fallen? ____________________

   ____

4. What is your song? ____________________

   ____

5. How might it be found again in the heart of a friend? ____________________

   ____

6. On the back of this paper, write your own song lyrics or poem; rhyming is not necessary. You may also choose to draw an artistic interpretive illusion. You decide on a topic. It's best to express whatever is on your mind but if you want ideas, try one of these:
   - Write to or about a friend.
   - Describe or depict what friendship is and isn't.
   - Think about, write or draw boomerang effects.
   - Discuss or illustrate love, hate, jealousy, grudges, forgiveness, random acts of kindness, etc.

Found Again

FOR THE FACILITATOR

I. Purpose

To consider the far-reaching influences of actions and words.

II. General Comments

Teens will see that seemingly random acts may hurt or help others or themselves.

III. Possible Activities

a. Write on the board *The Arrow and the Song*; ask what comes to mind (teens may recognize the Longfellow poem title; an *arrow* may be a weapon; a *song* may convey thoughts and feelings).

b. Distribute the *Found Again* handout and ask a few teens to read the poem aloud.

c. Explain that there are no right or wrong interpretations. People experience poetry each in their own way.

d. Discuss what the poet might mean by an arrow (a mean remark or cruel act; an idea or goal, etc.).

e. Ask how a song differs from an arrow (an arrow is an actual object; a song is abstract – its message is seen by the mind's eye, its beauty is heard, its emotions are felt).

f. Ask the significance of *It fell to earth I knew not where* (the author did not know the destination of the arrow or song; people do not know the possible future effects of their ideas, words and actions).

g. Ask what might be meant by … *in an oak I found the arrow, still unbroke* (the arrow's strength remained, possibly a great idea spread; possibly a hurt that stayed with the person).

h. Ask teens their thoughts about … *And the song, from beginning to end, I found again in the heart of a friend.*
Examples: love, generosity, kindness, friendship, etc. eventually returned to the author.

i. Ask whether the author thought the arrow or song would be found or returned.
Elicit concepts
- We never know the impact of our ideas, behavior or words on others.
- Effects on others are often penetrating.
- While we do not give, in order to receive in return, people usually treat us as we treat them.
- Consequences come back to haunt us; rewards return in unexpected ways.

j. Allow time for teens to complete the handout questions and to write lyrics or poems or to create an artistic interpretive illustration.

k. Encourage teens to share their responses and to real aloud their lyrics or poems.

IV. Enrichment Activities

a. Encourage teens to select a topic and brainstorm related words and phrases.

b. A volunteer lists the ideas on the board.

c. Suggest using all their senses to describe sights, sounds, smells, sensations, etc. related to the topic.

d. Encourage teens to collaborate and compose a song or poem or an artistic interpretation using the words and phrases. Interpretive illustrations may be posted by the artists.

e. Another volunteer writes the lines of the song or poem on the board.

f. Another volunteer copies it onto paper.

g. Photocopy and distribute to the group.

Song Snippets

Playlist Team

Compose a list of your own about relationships.

1. ____________________
2. ____________________
3. ____________________
4. ____________________
5. ____________________
6. ____________________
7. ____________________
8. ____________________
9. ____________________
10. ____________________

Lyrics Team

Write lyrics you would like to say to a friend who hurt you:

Write lyrics you would like to say to a friend who helped you:

Words Worth Team

Brainstorm ten words related to friendship.

1. ____________________
2. ____________________
3. ____________________
4. ____________________
5. ____________________
6. ____________________
7. ____________________
8. ____________________
9. ____________________
10. ____________________

Write lyrics that include the above words.

Song Snippets

FOR THE FACILITATOR

I. Purpose

To stimulate thoughts and feelings about friendship through song lyrics.

II. General Comments

Music moves teens – actual songs as well as created playlists and their own compositions.

III. Possible Activities

a. Before session photocopy the *Song Snippets* handout and cut on the broken lines.
b. Write a few musical notes on the board and ask teens what emotions surface when they hear music. Elicit that music can fuel anger or depression, lift a mood and make one think.
c. Ask teens to brainstorm songs that affect them positively; a peer lists them on board.
d. Ask for examples of familiar songs about relationships and/or friendships and the messages they convey.
e. Divide the group into three teams; each team elects a person to write their ideas.
f. Provide each team with one of the cutouts and review the instructions with them.
g. Allow time for completion.
h. Teens re-convene and share their work with peers.
i. For each team's list and/or lyrics ask the following:
   - What message do you receive from these words?
   - What feelings do you experience?
   - How does this relate to your life experiences?

IV. Enrichment Activities

a. Encourage the group to write lyrics for the titles the Playlist Team developed.
   - Copy the playlist on the board.
   - The group, teams or individuals select a title and write related songs.
b. Encourage teens to write a group song about friendship, relationships, etc.
   - The first person writes the first line.
   - The paper is passed among all teens.
   - Each teen anonymously adds a line.
   - After all have added their lines, a volunteer reads the song aloud.
   - Encourage teens to compose a melody and/or dance steps that fit the lyrics.
c. Encourage teens to write a group poem about friendship with all questions or questions and answers.
   - The first person writes a question.
   - Each teen anonymously adds a question or answer.
   - After all have added their lines, a volunteer reads the song aloud.
   - Encourage teens to compose a melody and/or dance steps that fit the lyrics.
d. Assign homework: teens research friendship-related song lyrics from *A-Z Lyrics* or other resources and bring them to the next session. Encourage them to share appropriate selections.

   Ask teens the following
   - What message did the artist convey?
   - Did the artist mean it literally?
   - What else could it mean?
   - How did the song lyrics make you feel?
   - How can you relate the lyrics to your life experiences?

Color Me Jealous . . . or Not

Color the arrows and finish the sentences.
(use name codes)

The grass no longer looks greener because

____

____

____

I get green with envy when

____

____

____

I see red when the person

____

____

____

I feel blue about it because

____

____

____

This could be my golden opportunity to

____

____

____

I could be tickled pink that

____

____

____

Color Me Jealous... or Not

FOR THE FACILITATOR

I. Purpose

To heal from resentment toward people who have coveted qualities or possessions.

II. General Comments

Teens may begrudge others' success, popularity, looks, finances, academic or athletic performance, etc.

Guilt over feelings of ill will and dissatisfaction with one's own achievements usually result.

III. Possible Activities

a. Before session obtain crayons or colored markers in green, red, blue, gold, and pink.
b. Write on the board *Color Me Jealous ... or Not*. Explain that jealousy is an awareness of an advantage or something someone has, a desire to have it and begrudge the other person for having it.
c. Encourage a discussion about jealousy in literature or theater (i.e. the wicked stepmother who resented Snow White's beauty because she herself wanted to be *fairest of them all.*)
d. Ask teens *What hurts more and why – to be jealous of a person's possession like a car or to be jealous of a trait like popularity?"*
e. Distribute the *Color Me Jealous ... or Not* handout; retain the crayons or color markers until later.
f. Remind teens they will color the arrows and write their thoughts **after** the examples are discussed.
g. A few volunteers read the sentence starters and provide examples.
   Possibilities
   - I get green with envy when *(Name Code) wins an award.*
   - I see red (feel angry) when the person *poses for photos.*
   - I feel blue (sad) about it because *I didn't win.*
   - This could be my golden opportunity to *grow beyond begrudging.*
   - I could be tickled pink (glad) that *I have other abilities.*
   - The grass no longer looks greener because *I stopped comparing myself with someone else.*
h. Encourage teens to delve deeply rather then using superficial sentence completions; their work will be private unless they wish to share.
i. Distribute crayons or markers; allow time for completion.
j. There are no right or wrong ways to color but most will color the top arrow a solid green; then the next arrows red, blue and gold; pink can be a lighter shade of red; the last arrow, a pale green.
k. Encourage teens to share their responses within their comfort zones.
l. Encourage teens to brainstorm ways to overcome jealousy; a peer lists their ideas on board.
   Examples
   - Recognize jealousy may be natural but detrimental to your peace.
   - Decide you want to be able to celebrate others' successes.
   - Decide to be grateful for what you have.
   - Do your best but do not compare yourself with others (apples and oranges).
   - Know that jealousy involves blindness to your own positive traits.
   - Do what you love for its own value (not for an outcome).

IV. Enrichment Activities

a. Write on the board:
   Do not spoil what you have by desiring what you have not; remember that what you now have was once among the things you only hoped for. ~ Epicurus
b. Encourage teens to personalize the quote's message.

Lifesavers

The **ABC's** of saving lives during medical emergencies are **A**irway, **B**reathing and **C**irculation.
The **ABC's** of being a friend who supports people during an emotional crisis are **A**sk, **B**uoy and **C**onnect.

Know the **ABC's**:

Write a situation in which a friend might be in an emotional crisis, seems very depressed, or is talking about harming her/himself or someone else. (use name code)

____

____

____

What can you **ask** your friend?

____

____

____

How can you **buoy** (keep afloat) your friend?

____

____

____

How can you **connect** your friend with help?

____

____

____

Lifesavers

FOR THE FACILITATOR

I. Purpose

To recognize and intervene for a friend who is having an emotional crisis, seems to be depressed, or contemplating suicide and/or hurting someone.

II. General Comments

To help someone, especially someone in a crisis, is the supreme social skill.
Teens often reveal suicidal or homicidal ideation to peers.
Teens are encouraged to provide support and hope, not advice, and lead the peer to a trusted adult.

III. Possible Activities

a. If possible give each teen a lifesaver candy at the start of session.
b. Ask a volunteer to draw on the board; whisper to draw a life buoy or round life preserver.
c. Ask teens what was drawn and its purpose (life buoy or ring; to save a drowning person).
d. Ask about ways that teens may be in emotional trouble (depression and suicidal ideation or wanting to harm others; addictions, breakups, grief over a loved one, abusive relationships, etc.).
e. Tell teens they will explore ways to help when friends are in crisis.
f. Distribute the *Lifesavers* handout; teens read aloud the explanation and life preserver labels.
g. Allow time for completion; encourage teens to share their responses. See concepts below.

1. **A**sk the person:
   - What happened?
   - What are your feelings about it?
   - What are you thinking to do about it?
   - Are you thinking about hurting yourself?
   - Are you thinking about hurting someone else?
2. **B**uoy the person:
   - Listen calmly.
   - Accept the person's feelings.
   - Believe the person who talks about harming self or others.
   - Offer hope by suggesting that the person finds other ways to handle feelings.
   - Tell the person you care about him/her.
3. **C**onnect the person with help:
   - If you feel in danger, leave and head for a safe place. Call 911.
   - If necessary call 911 or your local emergency services number.
   - Do not promise secrecy.
   - Ask the person to tell a trusted adult.
   - Offer to be with the person who needs to tell a trusted adult.
   - Offer to go with the person to the nearest hospital's emergency department.
   - Help the person call the Suicide Hotline 1-800- 273-TALK (8255).
   - Stay with the person until the person tells a trusted adult (even if the hotline was called).
   - If the person will not seek help, immediately tell an adult (teacher, counselor, etc.).

IV. Enrichment Activities

a. Encourage a discussion of risk factors like substance abuse, mental illness, feeling rejected.
b. Encourage a discussion of danger signs like talking or writing about death, weapons, reckless behavior, guilt, extreme anger, giving away possessions, mood swings, missing school or work, unexplained bruises, a sudden sense of calm in a person who has been upset, or increased energy in a depressed person.

Family life is not a computer program that runs on its own;
it needs continual input from everyone.

~ Neil Kurshan

Fam-Mobile

Place a check in front of the statement that best describes your family style.

1. _____ Single parent
2. _____ Stepfamily
3. _____ Two biological parents
4. _____ Adoptive family
5. _____ Foster family
6. _____ Grandparents or other relatives as caregivers
7. _____ Group home leaders
8. _____ Other (Describe) ______________________

____

A. What are the advantages of your family style?

____

____

B. What are the disadvantages of your family style?

____

____

C. What have you learned from your family about getting along with people?

____

____

D. What do you wish was different within your family?

____

____

A family is like a mobile moving in the wind;
when one member changes the others are affected.

What positive changes can you make?

Thoughts	Words	Actions
Ex: "I can accept my step-parent."	*Ex: "Can I help with that project?"*	*Ex: Do part of the work.*

Fam-Mobile

FOR THE FACILITATOR

I. Purpose

To identify lessons learned at home about getting along with people.

To empower teens to be the change-makers in their families, regardless of others' reactions.

II. General Comments

Teens are helped to see their role in potential family change; teens gain social skills regardless of the family's response.

III. Possible Activities

a. If possible show a crib mobile or wind chimes; ask a teen to pull or push one of the characters.
b. Ask teens what happens when a piece of the mobile or wind chimes moves (the others move).
c. Ask teens how this resembles a family (what one member does affects the others).

Family-Style Team Activity Option

- Distribute the *Fam-Mobile* handout and ask teens to check the description that best fits their family.
- Ask teens with similar family styles to sit together as teams.
- Each team elects a writer to record their responses (all on one handout per team).
- Teammates brainstorm ideas for A, B, C, D, and the Thoughts, Words and Action boxes.
- Teams re-convene; writers share their teams' responses.
- Ask teens if their changes guarantee that other family members will change (no).
- Ask what teens gain through positive thoughts, words and actions regardless of the family outcomes. (Social skills; the knowledge that they did their part to improve a situation).
- Encourage teens to compare and contrast the different family styles within the group.
- For styles not represented in the group, ask teens how they think people within those families would answer.

Individual Option

- Distribute the *Fam-Mobile* handout to each teen; allow time for completion.
- Encourage teens to share their responses and receive peer feedback.

Possible responses for team or individual options:

Family Type	Advantages	Disadvantages	What is Learned	Wish to Change
1. Single parent	One leader	One breadwinner	Help each other	More money
2. Stepfamily	Parent is not alone	New members	Adapt to change	Consistent rules
3. Two biological parents	Shared genes and medical history	Disagreements	Compromise	Less conflict
4. Adoptive family	They chose me	Siblings are parents' bio-kids	Expect equal treatment	Less rivalry
5. Foster family	They went to parenting classes	Miss biological parents	Live by the rules	More privileges
6. Grandparents or relatives	Family ties	Old-fashioned	Respect different views	Rules in tune with modern times
7. Group home leaders	Leaders chose this position	Somewhat impersonal	People come and go from our lives	More long-term relationships
8. Other				

IV. Enrichment Activities

Encourage a discussion about related topics.

Examples

- What information should adoptees receive about biological parents and at what age?
- What roles do you think are usually carried out by the eldest, middle and youngest child? Explain.

Sib-Rival Survival Conflict

Power	Individuality	Personal Space	Comparison	Favoritism
Birth Order	Temperament	Victimization	Sharing	Inequality

Label the teen/sibling issues below with the conflict category from above.

1. ______________________ Sibling is bossy.
2. ______________________ Sibling gets a bigger allowance.
3. ______________________ Teen is labeled the *baby of the family.*
4. ______________________ Teen is often put down by the sibling.
5. ______________________ Teen doesn't knock before entering the sibling's room.
6. ______________________ Teen's taste in music is very different than the sibling's.
7. ______________________ Family asks why the teen can't be more like the sibling.
8. ______________________ Teen likes it quiet at home; the sibling brings loud people home.
9. ______________________ Sibling gets away with behavior that the other gets disciplined for.
10. ______________________ Sibling plays on the computer when the teen needs to do homework.

What are the **advantages** of **having no siblings**?

____

____

____

What are the **disadvantages** of **having no siblings**?

____

____

____

What are the **advantages** of **having siblings**?

____

____

____

What are the **disadvantages** of **having siblings**?

____

____

____

(Continued on page 95)

Sib-Rival Survival Conflict

FOR THE FACILITATOR

I. Purpose

To identify sibling rivalry issues; to apply related skills to life situations.

II. General Comments

Equality and fairness, personal domain and identity are common areas of contention.

III. Possible Activities

a. Before session photocopy the *Sib-Rival Survival Conflict* handout, page 93.

b. Write on the board *Is life always fair?* (no) Ask teens *Why?* (abilities, needs and situations differ).

c. Ask about sources of conflict between siblings.

d. Distribute the handout to teens and allow time for completion.

e. Encourage teens to share responses.

Possibilities

1. Power
2. Favoritism or Inequality
3. Birth Order
4. Victimization
5. Personal Space
6. Individuality
7. Comparison
8. Temperament
9. Favoritism or Inequality
10. Sharing

Sib-Rival Survival Situations

(Continued from page 93)

Many life situations are similar to sibling rivalry.

1. What can you do if someone receives more recognition?

2. How can you handle a power-hungry person?

3. How can you get along with someone whose interests are different?

4. How can you respect a person's privacy?

5. How can you handle a situation in which someone receives more privileges?

6. How can you get along with someone who is your opposite, regarding shy or outgoing?

7. What can you tell yourself when someone compares you to somebody else?

8. How can you make sure you don't exclude people?

9. How can you handle a bullying situation?

10. What do you usually want to keep to yourself that you might share in a particular situation?

Sib-Rival Survival Situations

FOR THE FACILITATOR *(Continued from page 94)*

Talk Show Format

- Set scenario of a talk show with teens as a panel.
- Select a volunteer as the talk show host.
- Provide the talk show host with a copy of *Sib-Rival Survival Situations* handout, page 95.
- The host asks the first question; peers give opinions (as the panel of "experts").
- Teens take turns playing host and members of the panel.
- Possible panel responses:

1. Applaud the person outwardly; recognize your own strengths inwardly.
2. Pick your battles and let the person win some; be assertive about important issues.
3. Learn about the person's interests; share ideas about your passions.
4. Knock; don't eavesdrop or read emails or texts; don't ask personal questions.
5. Consider whether privileges were earned; prove your ability to handle responsibility.
6. Celebrate each other's differences; compromise if you share space.
7. Know you're a unique individual, one who does not try to be like somebody else.
8. Include bystanders in conversations; invite newcomers to join in activities, etc.
9. Ask the bully to stop (if safe); tell parent/caregivers about a sibling; anonymously tell trusted adults.
10. Answers will vary: time, attention, material items, compliments, acts of kindness, etc.

Individual Format

- Distribute copies of the two handouts, *Sib-Rival Survival Conflict*, page 93 and *Sib-Rival Survival Situations*, page 95.
- Allow time for completion; encourage teens to share responses.

IV. Enrichment Activities

a. Ask teens how twins or same sex siblings close in age develop their own identities.

Possibilities

Different friends, interests, activities, goals, appearances, personalities, values.

b. Ask for a show of hands of teens who have no siblings.

c. Then ask for a show of hands of teens who have siblings (including biological, steps, halfs and foster siblings).

d. Ask for volunteers to share how their situation works for them.

Power Figures

Think about your family or caregivers authority figures.
Draw and/or describe times you reacted in the following ways:

SHRINK Cower in Fear	**STOMP** Fight Back	**STAND** Act Assertively

What happens if you fear people in power?

____

____

What happens if you try to stomp on them?

____

____

How can you respectfully *stand in place* (neither back down nor step on their toes)?

____

____

Power Figures

FOR THE FACILITATOR

I. Purpose

To neither fear nor rebel against authority.

To respect authority while maintaining self-respect.

II. General Comments

Teens in the process of developing individuality and independence often have difficulty with authority. If their early caregivers were punitive, teens may fear or resent people in power. If they had few rules at home, teens may resent following a system in which regulations are imposed. Those from a democratic home may expect to have equal input everywhere.

III. Possible Activities

a. If possible, display actual toy figures or pictures from *Power Rangers* or *Star Wars* etc.
b. Ask teens to share thoughts about their favorite power figures.
c. Ask *Who are the family/caregiver power figures in your life?*
d. Ask for examples of power figures who themselves come under a higher authority.
   Possibilities
   - A teacher is under the principal who is under the board of education.
   - An older sibling who still needs to listen to parents.
e. Reinforce that throughout life people come under authority of one kind or another.
f. Ask teens to brainstorm ways people respond to authority figures.
   Possibilities
   - *Shrink* – Cower in fear
   - *Stomp* – Fight back
   - *Stand* – Act assertively
   - Manipulate *(Give me what I want or I'll ...)*
   - Divide and conquer (create conflict among powerful people to weaken to their strength)
g. Distribute the *Power Figures* handout and allow time for completion.
h. Remind teens that artistic skill does not matter; they may use stick figures, symbols, cartoons, etc.
i. Encourage teens to share their drawings and responses and to receive peer feedback.
j. Discuss that to fear a person in power prevents teens' growth; to trample results in consequences.
k. Elicit ways to *stand in place* with an authority figure; a volunteer lists ideas on board.
l. **Examples**
   - Politely ask questions, listen and state your views.
   - Do not blame.
   - Tell the truth.
   - Realize the person is human, not superhuman (to diminish intimidation).
   - Remember that you have rights to meet your needs.
   - Seek help if you are too needy of approval from authority figures.
   - Enlist a trusted adult to mediate if your needs are ignored or put down.

IV. Enrichment Activities

a. Encourage teens to demonstrate the *empty chair technique* wherein they practice acting aassertive in an upcoming encounter with an authority figure; peers provide feedback.
b. Ask teens to prepare mock videos (role plays) showing how **to** and how **not to** respond to authority.
c. Plan other sessions and suggest other categories of authoritative figures to focus on, such as school personnel, volunteer or work supervisors. Photocopy a separate *Power Figure* handout, page 97, for each category. You may white out the reference to *family or caregivers* in the first line of text and substitute *school personnel, volunteer or work supervisors* or other categories for future sessions.

Riddles

Make up riddles whose answers are *Teens*.

Example: Whose thumbs are sore from texting? (Answer: Teens)

1. ______
2. ______
3. ______
4. ______
5. ______
6. ______
7. ______
8. ______
9. ______

Riddles

Make up riddles whose answers are *Adults*.

Example: Who still uses snail mail? (Answer: Adults)

1. ______
2. ______
3. ______
4. ______
5. ______
6. ______
7. ______
8. ______
9. ______

Riddles

Make up riddles whose answers are *Wise People*.

Example: Who loves video games but waits until work is done, plays, and then gets enough sleep? (Answer: Wise People)

1. ______
2. ______
3. ______
4. ______
5. ______
6. ______
7. ______
8. ______
9. ______

(Continued on page 101)

Riddles

FOR THE FACILITATOR

I. Purpose

To forgive others and self; to practice the steps of an apology.

II. General Comments

Teens will recognize that forgiveness is important for mental health and relationships. The first page of the handout is a fun warm-up activity; the second page links teens, adults, and wise people to forgiveness.

III. Possible Activities

a. Before session photocopy the *Riddles* handout.

b. For the **Team Format**, cut the first page, *Riddles*, Page 99, on the broken lines (one third of the page for each of three teams); make, but retain, enough copies of the second page for all participants.

c. For the **Individual Format**, do not cut the first page, *Riddles*, Page 99, and make enough copies of both pages, *Riddles*, Page ____, and *Riddles – A Quotation*, Page 101, for all participants. (The *Riddles* page will be used for warm-up; the *Riddles Quotation* page later).

d. When session begins ask teens to share a few riddles they have heard.

e. Explain they will make up funny or serious riddles related to teens, adults and wise people.

Team Format

- Divide into three teams; each receives the Teens, Adults or Wise People cutout from the first page.
- Retain the second page until later.
- Teammates sit together and brainstorm riddles; a writer records their ideas onto the cutout list.
- Teens re-unite and the writers share their teams' riddles.

Individual Format

- Distribute the first page, uncut, and direct teens to write riddles for each (Teens, Adults and Wise People).
- Encourage teens to share their riddles.

Both Formats

f. After the riddles have been shared, distribute the second page of the handout.

g. Ask a volunteer to read the quotation aloud.

h. Allow time for completion.

i. Encourage teens to share their responses. Concepts to elicit are suggested below.

1. Why forgive?

   Possibilities
   - To help overcome resentment.
   - To stop the desire to get even.
   - Because the relationship is more important than the mistake.
   - To show compassion.
   - To ensure good mental health (not forgiving adds to anxiety and depression).
   - To help physical health (holding grudges may worsen some conditions and cause new pain).
   - Because we all have made mistakes and want to be forgiven.
   - To be aware that we can forgive even if we do not forget.

2. Apology completions will be personalized.
   - Discuss the format and suggest that teens save the page for future apologies.
   - Teens may wish to write letters of apology.

3. Checklist completions will be personalized.
   - Suggest that teens keep the page to remember the self-forgiveness steps.
   - Encourage teens to discuss the fact that our apologies are not always accepted but trying to right a wrong helps us know we have done what we can to restore the relationship.

(See page 102 Riddles for the Facilitator*, continued - IV - Enrichment Activities)*

Riddles – A Quotation *(Continued)*

The day the child realizes that all adults are imperfect, he becomes an adolescent;
the day he forgives them, he becomes an adult;
the day he forgives himself, he becomes wise.

~ Alden Nowlan

1. Why forgive?

____

____

2. Complete one or more of the apologies below to someone you wronged:

I was wrong when I ______________________________.

I know I caused you pain by ______________________________.

I am sorry for ______________________________.

Please forgive me for ______________________________.

I will take these actions to restore your trust: ______________________________

____

______________________________.

3. Self-forgiveness Checklist

- ❑ I admitted I was wrong.
- ❑ I acknowledged I caused pain.
- ❑ I expressed regret.
- ❑ I asked for forgiveness.
- ❑ I am working to restore trust in specific ways.
- ❑ I have asked for spiritual guidance if needed.
- ❑ I forgive myself.

Riddles

FOR THE FACILITATOR ***(Continued from page 100)***

IV. Enrichment Activities

a. Ask teens to brainstorm reasons some people will not forgive.
   - They like the *victim* role.
   - They want the offender to owe them.
   - They feel in control when they can *hold it over someone's head.*
   - They want to feel superior to the offender.
   - They want revenge.
   - They are energized by anger.
   - They think forgiving is a sign of weakness.
   - They think the offender is not sincere.
   - They think the offender will not change.
   - They do not realize that even though they forgive, they do not necessarily forget.

b. Discuss situations where teens were wronged and the offender did not apologize.
   - Reinforce the need to forgive for teens' own peace of mind.
   - Elicit that hatred hurts teens more than the persons who wronged them.

c. Write on the board or photocopy the following quotes and encourage teens to personalize each.

This is certain, that a man that studies revenge keeps his wounds green, which otherwise would heal and do well.

~ Francis Bacon

When you haven't forgiven those who've hurt you, you turn back against your future. When you do forgive, you start walking forward.

~ Tyler Perry

To err is human; to forgive divine.

~ Alexander Pope

Forgiveness is a gift you give to yourself.

~ Tony Robbins

TEEN LOVE 6

Love is a little blind. When we love someone dearly, we unconsciously overlook so many thoughts.

~ Beatrice Saunders

First Date

Guess what the hints below tell you about making a hit with parents or caregivers.

If your date is for a prom, what touchy topic might a corsage cause?

How might you get around the corsage dilemma?

What clues below tell you your date might want a kiss?

What body language says to back off?

Circle the speech balloons that might lead to another date.

I … My … I … My…

What are your favorite movies, songs …?

Why did you and your ex break-up?

Let's talk about politics.

Tell me about your career plans.

Excuse me while I answer my messages.

What are your ideas about …?

Guess what I heard about someone …

What a great body that person has!

First Date

FOR THE FACILITATOR

I. Purpose

To consider acceptable dating practices and ways to win favor with dating partners and caregivers.

II. General Comments

Courtesies, clues, conversation and safety are addressed.

III. Possible Activities

a. Ask teens to share the most difficult aspects of a first date.
b. Explain that teens will first do an activity about dating and then discuss their ideas.
c. Distribute the *First Date* handout and allow time for completion.
d. Encourage teens to share their responses.

Concepts to elicit

- The person who is driving is expected to go to the date's door and meet the parents or caregivers.
- Teens make a hit with adults when they ask what time they need to be home and adhere to the curfew.
- To pin a corsage on a female's dress is *touchy*.
- Solve the problem with wrist corsage.
- Clues about a kiss include eye contact and making lips available; turn toward the person, smile.
- Body language that says to back off: turn away, step back, avoid eye contact, act in a hurry to leave.
- Speech balloons that lead to future dates are open-ended questions about neutral topics: *What are your favorite…? Tell me about your career plans. What are your ideas about …?*

e. Ask teens reasons to avoid all the other speech balloons.

Concepts to elicit

- *I … My …* because it's NOT all about me. Showing interest in one's date is preferable.
- Politics are too controversial and reasons for a past break-up are too personal for a first date.
- Gossip is never acceptable.
- To answer phone messages diminishes the partner's importance.
- To comment about another's body undermines the date's appearance.

IV. Enrichment Activities

Pose other questions about first dates.

Possible responses are parenthesized.

a. If your date is paying for your meal, how do you know what the person can afford? (Choose within the same price range).
b. How do you know what to wear? (Ask where you are going or ask if casual or dressy clothes are expected).
c. What do you say at the end of a date? (*Thank you, I had a good time*; say *I'll call you* ONLY if you mean it).
d. What activities are recommended for first dates? (Plan to be in public places for safety reasons: movies, restaurants, concerts, plays, sporting events, dances, busy parks or beaches).
e. If the person drinks, uses drugs, has a weapon or pressures you for sex, what do you do? (Have a back-up plan for getting home safely – call your parent, caregiver, or trusted adult. Have an emergency code word, etc.).

Parent / Caregiver Concerns

Reasons your parents or caregivers might disapprove of your partners:

1. There is a racial difference.
2. You are isolating yourself from your friends
3. You have different religious backgrounds.
4. You eat too much (or too little).
5. Your partner acts possessive.
6. Your partner has a disability.
7. Your partner had unprotected sex.
8. Your partner encourages or pressures you to indulge in an addiction.
9. Your grades are falling.
10. Your partner plays mind games with you like flirting with another person in front of you.
11. Your partner's appearance (hair styles, piercings, clothes).
12. Your partner is causing you bodily harm.
13. Your partner has friends who take dangerous risks.
14. Your partner has a quick temper.
15. Your partner shows extreme jealousy.
16. You have stopped activities, clubs, sports or groups you previously enjoyed.
17. Your partner drives recklessly.
18. You act against your own beliefs.
19. There is a cultural difference between you and your partner.
20. Your mood depends on your partner's mood.
21. Your partner is self-centered.
22. You have problems sleeping.
23. Your partner puts you down privately and in public.
24. Your partner forces sex.
25. You are blind to your partner's faults.
26. You and your partner's economic status is very different.
27. Your partner is the same sex as you.
28. Your partner tries to control you.
29. There is a huge age difference between you and your partner.
30. Your partner is physically, verbally, emotionally and/or sexually abusive.

Place the number of the concern under the heading that best describes it.

Partner Traits	Changes in You	Debatable Concerns

Circle YOUR concerns. How will you handle these situations? ______________________

____

____

____

Parent/Caregiver Concerns

FOR THE FACILITATOR

I. Purpose

To consider parent/caregiver apprehensions about dating partners; to recognize valid concerns.

II. General Comments

Most adult worries relate to potential emotional, physical and academic consequences of intense or unhealthy relationships. Sometimes bigotry and reluctance to let the teen grow up are involved.

III. Possible Activities

Board Activity

- Before session photocopy the *Parent/Caregiver Concerns* handout.
- The handout is the teens' master copy.
- Number 30 index cards or scraps of paper – 1 through 30. Shuffle and place face down in a pile.
- Copy the handout's table and headings onto the board; place the handout near the pile of numbers.
- Start the session by asking about reasons parents/caregivers may disapprove of teens' partners (accept any responses).
- Explain that teens take turns going to the front of the room, pick up a cutout and read aloud the corresponding item from the master copy. *Ex:* for #5 the teen reads *"Your partner acts possessive"* aloud.
- The teen asks peers under which heading the statement belongs and writes the words in that column. Ex: teen prints *"Acts possessive"* under **Partner Traits** on the board.
- Some statements may apply to more than one heading; accept any answers teens can substantiate.
- Encourage discussion and debate.
- Ask volunteers to share which items apply to their situations.

Individual Activity

- Start the session by asking about reasons parents/caregivers may disapprove of teens' partners (accept any responses).
- Distribute the *Parent/Caregiver Concerns* handout to teens and allow time for completion.
- Encourage teens to share their responses; encourage discussion and debate.

Possibilities

Partner Traits	Changes in Teen	Debatable Concerns
5, 7, 8, 10, 12, 13, 14, 15, 17, 21, 23, 24, 28, 29, 30	2, 4, 9, 16, 18, 20, 22, 25	1, 3, 6, 11, 19, 26, 27

IV. Enrichment Activities

Encourage a discussion about ways to handle criticisms of the partner or relationship.

Possibilities

a. Listen and decide whether their concerns are valid. Examine your motives – Are you being rebellious or thinking that having a partner will make you popular? Are you in denial about drawbacks?
b. If bigotry is involved, state your opinion and then ask if you can agree to disagree and discuss calmly.
c. Tell parents/caregivers about your partner's positive qualities.
d. Arrange for parents/caregivers and your partner to get to know each other.
e. Seek help from a trusted adult, counselor or spiritual advisor if you are being abused, obsessed with the person, emotionally stressed, depressed or suicidal, or if you are abusing someone or substances.

Love-U Bingo – First Love

My First Love ________________
NAME CODE

L 1-10	O 11-20	V 21-30	E 31-40	U 41-50
Share thoughts about your first date.	If you broke up, what were the reasons?	What traits about the person did you try not to see?	Share thoughts about the places that remind you of the person.	What did your family say about this first love?
Share thoughts about your most meaningful date.	In what ways was the relationship healthy?	What did you learn from the relationship?	How have you changed because of the relationship?	What did your friends say about this person?
Tell about what happened the last time you saw the person.	In what ways was the relationship unhealthy?	What personality traits attracted you to the person?	Explain the relationship's level of togetherness.	Share song lyrics or a poem that reminds you of your first love.
Share memories about your first argument.	How strong was the physical attraction?	If you broke up, how did you handle it?	Did you usually put the person first or yourself first? Explain.	What reminds you of the person?
How did you work things out after your first argument?	Explain what you gave up for the person. Was it worth it?	Discuss the level of honesty or dishonesty between you and the person.	What did the person tell you about yourself? Is it true?	Were you able to remain friends?

Love-U Bingo – Current Love

My Current Love ___________________
NAME CODE

L 1-10	O 11-20	V 21-30	E 31-40	U 41-50
Describe the level of security you feel in the relationship.	What values do you have in common?	About what do you usually agree?	About what do you usually disagree?	How do you usually resolve conflicts?
How do you get along with each other's families?	How do you get along with each other's friends?	When you disagree, do you 'fight fair'?	How can you treat the person better?	How can the person treat you better?
In what ways have you positively influenced the person?	In what ways have you negatively influenced the person?	In what ways has the person positively influenced you?	In what ways has the person negatively influenced you?	What beliefs do you stick to despite pressure to do otherwise?
What will you not tolerate in this relationship?	What do you respect about this person?	What have you given up to please this person?	What do you NOT respect about this person?	Does this person make your problems less or more stressful? How?
How have your grades been affected by this relationship?	How have your extracurricular activities been affected by this relationship?	How has your self-esteem been affected by this relationship?	Are you able to say NO to this person?	What would you do if physical, verbal, emotional or sexual abuse occurred?

Love-U Bingo – Future Loves

L 1-10	O 11-20	V 21-30	E 31-40	U 41-50
Describe the personality traits you would like in a new love.	In what ways will you be a good partner?	About what beliefs will you not compromise?	In what ways are you a giving person?	What quality do you like best about yourself?
How important are a person's looks?	In what ways will you show respect?	About what issues can you compromise?	How are you going about meeting a new person to date?	Where or how can you find a like-minded person?
What common interests would you like to have?	Do you prefer constant contact or a degree of separation? Explain.	How important is your family's approval of a person?	What behaviors turn you off?	What is your idea of a healthy relationship?
What values do you hope the person has?	How important to you is sex or no sex in a relationship?	How much do your friends influence you about someone you date?	Describe your idea of a great first date.	What is your idea of an unhealthy relationship?
How important is the person's religion or spirituality to you?	In what ways are you sometimes selfish?	In a prior relationship, how were you supportive to the person?	If you had a prior relationship, how did you hurt the person?	What qualities will a person's family like about you?

Love-U Bingo

FOR THE FACILITATOR

I. Purpose

To consider healthy and unhealthy aspects of teens' first, current and/or future romantic relationships.

II. General Comments

First love leaves a lifelong impression, current relationships consume much attention and foresight may lead to favorable future partnerships.

III. Possible Activities

a. Before session photocopy several of each of the *Love-U Bingo* pages, 109, 110 and 111.
b. Write *First Love, Current Love* and *Future Loves* on the board.
c. Explain that teens will play *Love-U* which is a bingo game.
d. Each teen will choose which card to play.

Suggestions

- Teens who wish to focus on their first love may choose *First Love.*
- Teens involved in a significant current relationship may choose *Current Love.*
- Teens who prefer not to focus on past or current relationships (or who have not yet been in a relationship) may choose *Future Loves*; teens play only one card each.

e. Distribute the LOVE-U handouts (cards) according to each teen's choice.
f. Instruct teens to randomly number the boxes (according to the ranges next to each letter).
g. Ideally everyone's numbers will be in different order.

Examples

Under L – a teen will label the boxes 1-10 in any order.
Under O – 11-20 in any order.
Under V – 21-30 in any order.
Under E – 31-40 in any order.
Under U – 41-50 in any order.

Alternately the facilitator or a volunteer numbers the pages differently before group.

h. Facilitator makes a blank bingo grid to write in the numbers as they 'call' them.
i. The Love-U Game
   - Facilitator calls one number per letter; teens with the number raise hands.
   - Teens read aloud their questions or directives and respond; no rights or wrongs.
   - If a teen cannot respond to the question or directive peers may assist.
   - After responding, teens color or mark an "X" in the corresponding box.
   - If the same teens continue to have lucky numbers, let those who have had no turns call the next numbers (using numbers they have on their pages).
   - Teens win by answering and marking all the boxes in a row horizontally, vertically or diagonally.
   - When someone wins, winner calls the numbers as peers continue to play.
   - At the session's end, if no one won, the teen(s) with the most marked numbers wins.

IV. Enrichment Activities

Write the following quotes on the board and encourage discussion and debate:

> ***There's no love like the first.*** ~ Nicholas Sparks
>
> ***Sometimes the heart sees what is invisible to the eye.*** ~ H. Jackson Brown Jr.

Pen Your Passion

Haiku

Haiku – has three lines with five, seven and five syllables (traditionally dealing with nature). *Example:*

They walked home from school (5 syllables)
Through snow and rain and thunder (7 syllables)
Warmed without the sun. (5 syllables)

Acrostic

Acrostic – write a word vertically, then write the poem across; it need not rhyme. *Example* for *Crush:*

CRUSH

Consuming me
Reason went out the window
Under its spell
Sensations and senselessness
How to handle?

Name Acrostic

Name Acrostic – Write a name vertically. Use name code. *Example* for *My Partner Loves Sports – MPLS:*

MPLS

My eyes see your
Passion for the game
Loudly I cheer for you
Screaming silently "Love me too!"

Rhyme

Your poem may have a different pattern like alternate lines rhyming or whatever you choose.
Example with two rhyming lines or couplets:

First talk
First walk
First kiss
First bliss
Will we grow old together?
Will love go cold forever?

Free Verse

Free verse may rhyme or not and has no specific pattern. *Example* with no rhyming:

The Ring
A diamond ablaze for one
"Looks like an icicle" to the other.
They melted then froze.

Limerick

A limerick has an AABBA rhyming pattern. *Example:*
There once was a couple in **love** (A)
And all they ever thought **of** (A)
Was passion and **pain**. (B)
Love's loss and its **gain** (B)
Wielded its velvet **glove**. (A)

Pen Your Passion

FOR THE FACILITATOR

I. Purpose

To encourage expression about love and related themes.

II. General Comments

Teens may drop the notions that poetry is boring or needs to rhyme as they experiment with different forms.

Teens will write and/or draw on the back of the handout or on other paper.

III. Possible Activities

a. Write *Pen Your Passion* on the board; ask its meaning (write a letter, poem or lyrics, or draw a picture).

b. Explain teens will express emotions about romantic relationships.

c. Distribute the *Pen Your Passion* handout; volunteers read the different types and examples aloud.

Team Format

- Ask teens to divide into six teams according to the form of poetry they want to write.
- Teammates sit together and designate one person to write as they dictate
- They compose one or more poems, depending on time limits.
- The group reconvenes and team writers read aloud their teams' verses.

Individual Format

- Each teen selects a form and writes a poem.
- Teens may select additional forms and write more poems depending on time limits.
- Encourage teens to share their verses.

Art and Literature Combined

- If possible have color markers, crayons, paints and large paper available.
- Ask teens to draw a picture about their relationship.

Examples

The couple, people who try to pull them apart, etc.

The place where they met or broke up, etc.

A related object like a cell phone they hope their partner will call.

A memento like a ticket stub from a first date.

- Teens may draw about someone they hope to date or their ideal partner.
- After teens draw, encourage them to write descriptions using prose or a poetic form.
- Encourage teens to share their work.

IV. Enrichment Activities

a. Create an anthology of teens' work.

b. Use names or safeguard anonymity according to your teens' preferences or your organization's protocols.

c. Photocopy and distribute.

Dating Dilemmas

1. You want to date a certain person.	2. Your parents/caregivers do not like your partner.	3. You broke your promise and cheated on your partner.	4. You pressure your partner to do things he/she does not want to do.
5. You wonder what to talk about on a first date.	6. Someone often flirts with your partner.	7. Your partner pressures you to do things you don't want to do.	8. You have threatened or harmed your partner.
9. You are nervous about having dinner with members of your partner's family.	10. Your partner flirts with people.	11. Your partner hurts your feelings.	12. You want to break up with your partner.
13. Your friends do not like your partner.	14. You want an exclusive relationship but your partner wants you both to date others.	15. Your partner threatens or hurts you physically.	16. Your partner breaks up with you.
17. Your partner does not like your friends.	18. Your partner agreed to date only you and cheated.	19. You say cruel things to your partner when you're angry.	20. You want to date your best friend's ex-partner.
21. You feel like half a person without your partner.	22. Your partner puts other activities ahead of time with you.	23. Your partner drinks and/or uses drugs and encourages you to do the same.	24. Because you are anxious about the relationship, you have started an addiction.
25. Your partner threatens to hurt you if you break up.	26. Your partner threatens suicide if you break up.	27. You feel like harming yourself or your partner.	28. Your partner falsely accuses you of cheating.

Dating Dilemmas

FOR THE FACILITATOR

I. Purpose

To develop social skills to cope with relationship issues.

II. General Comments

Teens play a game that reinforces positive ways to handle romantic challenges.

III. Possible Activities

a. Before session photocopy the *Dating Dilemmas* handout, page 115, cut-out the boxes, place face down in a container; make copies of the *Know "No"* handout, page 117, but retain for later (Enrichment Activities).

b. Ideally teens sit in a circle and take turns after the person sitting next to them.

c. Provide teens with paper and pencil to record the numbers of points they accrue.

d. Explain the game:

- A teen picks a cutout, reads aloud, states one positive way to handle the situation and records one point on his/her paper.
- The next teen states a second way and records two points; the third, fourth and fifth teens earn three, four and five points respectively and note their points (for a running tally as game goes on).
- After the first dilemma, teens continue to take turns picking up cutouts and suggesting coping skills; teens accrue one for the first and up to five points for the fifth responses to each cutout.
- After all cutouts are used, the teen with the most points wins.

Examples of positive responses

1. Ask what the person likes to do. Suggest going out with a group of friends. Ask a friend to invite you both to a party. Go places where the person hangs out. Talk on social media.
2. Ask reasons. Listen with an open mind. State why you like your partner. Help the partners and caregivers get to know each other. Try to compromise.
3. Ask yourself if you wanted to cause jealousy. Admit your mistake. Ask for forgiveness. Discuss whether both of you want to date other people (plus each other). Decide whether to break up.
4. Stop pressuring. Accept *No.* Ask yourself if you're being selfish. Try to understand your partner's reasons. Suggest a compromise if appropriate.
5. Comment about the place you met (school, work). Ask about interests. Share thoughts about your activities. Discuss favorites (music, movies). Comment on the current pop culture events.
6. See if your partner flirts back. Share your concerns with your partner. Trust your partner. Ignore it. If the flirter is a friend explain to your friend that it makes you uncomfortable.
7. Say *"No."* Explain your reasons. Ask your partner to respect your wishes. Use instant replay (after each request refuse with the same words like *I won't,* etc.). Agree to disagree and move on.
8. Apologize. Tell a trusted adult. Respect your partner's wishes (probably to break up). Accept responsibility for your actions. Do not blame your partner. Seek help for anger management.
9. Ask about their occupations. Ask about their interests. Compliment the food. Comment about art work or other decorative items. Discuss local news (avoid politics and religion).
10. Explain how it affects you. Ask your partner to stop, If your partner insists the flirting is harmless decide if you can accept it or not. Determine if you are overly sensitive or your partner is insensitive.
11. Explain how you feel *(I feel ______ when ______________).* Ask your partner to stop. Consider ending the relationship if the put downs continue. Decide if your feelings are hurt too easily or if your partner is cruel.
12. Break up in person (if safe) or talk on the phone (do not text or email). Do not blame your partner. Tactfully explain why (this may help the person in future relationships). Comment about your partner's positive qualities. Discuss whether a clean break or a friendship will work in your situation.

See page 118 for Dating Dilemmas for the Facilitator (III Possible Activities, continued, and IV Enrichment Activities

Dating Dilemmas
Know "No"

Techniques to say "No"	Examples:
1. Understand and then emphasize your *"No."*	*A. "No, I'm not willing to do that".*
2. Instant replay.	*B. "You and I feel differently about this. Let's hope we can agree to disagree."*
3. Just say *"No."*	*C "Please respect my wishes."*
4. Apologize if appropriate.	*D. "If you cared about me you wouldn't pressure me."*
5. Explain your reasons if appropriate.	*E. "Let's not be home alone anymore."*
6. Respond to *"If you cared about me you would…"*	*F. "I recognize your frustration however I am not able to do it."*
7. Share your feelings.	*G. "It is against my beliefs."*
8. Make a request.	*H. "I feel stressed when you keep asking."*
9. Avoid situations where you could be tempted to give in.	*I. "I'm sorry this upsets you but I can't."*
10. Agree to disagree.	*J. Listen to the requests then repeatedly say* "I won't" *or* "No" *after each request.*

Next to each technique's number place the corresponding example's letter below.

1. ______
2. ______
3. ______
4. ______
5. ______
6. ______
7. ______
8. ______
9. ______
10. ______

Which technique(s) do you like best? ________________________________ Explain:

____

____

____

Dating Dilemmas

FOR THE FACILITATOR *(continued from page 116)*

III. Possible Activities and IV. Enrichment Activities *(Continued)*

13. Find out why. Determine if their reasons make sense. Listen but make up your own mind. Arrange time with friends away from your partner. Agree to disagree about your partner.
14. Agree to date others. Keep an open mind about new people. Decide if your feelings are much stronger than your partner's. Decide whether to continue this relationship or break-up.
15. Tell a trusted adult. Break up in a safe way, with friends or family near. Suggest anger management. Seek counseling to help you recover. Recognize signs of abuse in the future.
16. Know you will be sad for a time but will be stronger. If partner blames you, consider your actions and decide if you agree. Know if it's not your fault - people grow in different ways. Seek support from friends and family. Do activities you loved before you were in a partnership. Do not check out what your ex is doing via social media or gossip.
17. Find out why. Decide if the reasons make sense. Determine if your partner wants to isolate you from friends (possessiveness). Spend time with friends away from your partner. Spend adequate time (but not all of your time) alone with your partner.
18. Decide if your partner acts sorry (admits it, asks for forgiveness), decide whether you believe and then forgive. Either give the person another chance or end the relationship if you cannot rebuild trust. Take time out from the relationship to think or to get counseling about the issue.
19. Count to ten or higher to think before you speak. Consider the consequences. Talk to someone you trust. Journal or draw your feelings.
20. Ask your friend and watch for body language as well as words. Decide against it if your friend still has feelings. Be sure the relationship is really over. Date the ex if the relationship was long ago or they have no lingering feelings for each other.
21. Develop your whole self. Decide what you like, dislike, can do and/or want to learn. Find ways to help others.
22. Know you can't always be first. Be interested and/or attend the other person's activities. Develop your own outside interests. Discuss priorities with your partner. Talk with a trusted person.
23. Ask your partner to stop. Suggest counseling or rehab. Break up if it continues. Do not be tempted to drink or use drugs. Realize that eventually the substances will become your partner's priority.
24. Talk to a trusted person. Discuss troublesome issues with your partner. Consider counseling or rehab. Realize this might not be a good relationship for you.
25. Tell your and your partner's parents/caregivers. Do not stay in a relationship because of fear. Do not break up with the person in a secluded area. Speak with a teacher or counselor.
26. Tell your and your partner's parents/caregivers. Tell a teacher or counselor. Seek counseling regarding the best way to end the relationship. Call 911 or your local emergency services number. Do not stay with the person because of fear.
27. Tell a trusted person. Seek counseling. Consider the consequences. Call 911 or your local emergency number or a suicide hotline. Go to the closest hospital emergency room. Express feelings through writing or drawing,
28. Tell your partner you did not cheat. Decide if you gave the appearance of cheating. Determine whether your partner is too suspicious or if you are too flirtatious. Talk about what you both will and won't tolerate in a partnership.

IV. Enrichment Activities

a. Distribute the *Know "No"* handout, page 117, and ask participants to match the first and second columns. Allow time for completion.
   Answer Key: 1. F, 2. J, 3. A, 4. I, 5. G, 6. D, 7. H, 8. C, 9. E, 10. B
b. Ask teens to compose anonymous *Dating Dilemmas* on slips of paper; place slips in a container.
c. Play the same game (one to five points per positive way to handle each situation, etc.).

Freeze

1. One person looks at wrist watch while waiting; the other person arrives late. (FREEZE)

2. One person points at the other person during an argument. (FREEZE)

3. One person calls the other person on the cell phone; that person looks at caller ID and does not answer the phone. (FREEZE)

4. One person talks to the other person. Meanwhile, the other person texts. (FREEZE)

5. In the midst of a phone conversation, one person slams down the phone. (FREEZE)

6. One person leaves the other person standing alone and walks off with friends. (FREEZE)

7. A couple (Chris and Pat) encounter two friends of Chris and two friends of Pat.
   Both sets of friends motion for the couple to join them.
   The couple walks off with Chris' friends and leaves Pat's friends behind. (FREEZE)

8. Two people have an argument; one person stomps away; the other one follows. (FREEZE)

9. One person is exercising; the other tries to talk to that person at the same time. (FREEZE)

10. Two people are dancing; one person copies the other's moves. (FREEZE)

11. One person reaches to hold hands; the other one pulls away. (FREEZE)

12. One person has a sprained ankle; the other one holds the door open. (FREEZE)

Freeze

FOR THE FACILITATOR

I. Purpose

To evaluate the role of power in romantic relationships.

II. General Comments

Silent *freeze frames* show how the person with the least interest usually has the most power.

III. Possible Activities

a. Before session cut the *Freeze* handout on the broken lines and place cut-outs face down.
b. Write *Power* on the board and ask its meaning in relationships (to influence the partner's behavior to achieve one's own goals; to have control over what the partner needs, wants and fears).
c. Explain that teens will portray and view pantomimes where the actors freeze in place like statues.
d. Remind teens that in real life, onlookers can be wrong; do not judge based on appearances.
e. Emphasize that for purposes of this game when each performance's freeze occurs, audience will imagine what each actor is thinking and guess who has the most power in the relationship.
f. Pairs of teens take turns; they pick up a cut-out, perform and freeze in place.
g. A few scenes require additional actors; the pair will recruit these *extras*.
h. Questions to ask after each freeze frame:
   - What does the audience believe each actor is thinking and/or feeling?
   - What do the actors think and feel in their roles?
   - Who does the audience think has the most power?

   Power concepts to elicit (corresponding to the numbers on the cut-outs):
   1. Latecomers may believe their time is most important; they use time as the power of control.
   2. Persons who point (usually to blame) seem to have an authoritative role.
   3. The person who is disinterested in taking the call usually has the most power.
   4. The person who shows less interest in the face-to-face conversation seems to have more power.
   5. The person who hangs up in the midst of conflict seems to have more power.
   6. The one who is less interested in the partner than friends seems to have more power.
   7. The person who makes the decision about whose friends to hang out with has more power.
   8. The person who walks away shows less interest and more power; the follower appears needy.
   9. The one doing jumping jacks represents a person with self-development goals and more power.
   10. The leader has more power; the copier may tend to agree with the leader's decisions.
   11. The one who pulls away shows less interest and more power.
   12. The person in the helping role usually has more power.

i. Ask *If the person who is less interested holds more power, should the other play hard to get?* (No; as soon as the other is caught the chaser can still lose interest).
j. Explain most people have both dependence and independence needs; those who are too dependent need to find ways to meet their own needs; independent types may need closer connections.
k. Ask teens to brainstorm ways the person who cares more can try to equalize the power.

   Possibilities
   - Develop interests and friendships outside of the relationship.
   - Continue to meet others; you may find someone who wants more involvement with you.
   - Match your level of interest to the person's rather than being too serious too soon.
   - Share your limits, explain what you will not tolerate; leave the relationship if boundaries are violated.
   - Seek relationships with people who want the same level of involvement as you do.

IV. Enrichment Activities

Encourage a discussion regarding when to honestly share the intensity of your feelings and when to end an unbalanced relationship. (Allow enough time for the other person to develop stronger feelings and for you to see where the relationship is headed, etc.).

From Ashes

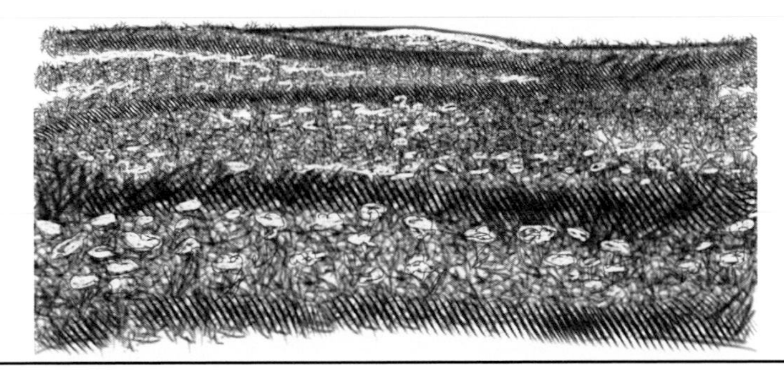

Forest fire ashes cause wildflowers to flourish.
Ashes represent the ruins of a romance unless —
I glean every bit of joy from the flame and growth from the pain.

1. Joys I will always remember: ______________________________

____

2. Pain I will never forget: ______________________________

____

3. I now will look for this in a relationship: ______________________________

____

4. I now know this about myself: ______________________________

____

5. The ruins can be *quicksand* if ______________________________

____

6. The ashes can be a *fertile ground* if ______________________________

____

7. I want these traits within me to thrive: ______________________________

____

8. Social media and electronics can help *weed out* connections to my ex if ______________________________

____

9. I will change my thinking to promote my growth.
   Example: *I'll never get over this* (strangles) to *This has made me wiser* (strengthens).

   Negative thought ______________________________

   Positive thought ______________________________

10. I loved and lost, yet from ashes ______________________________

____

From Ashes

FOR THE FACILITATOR

I. Purpose

To derive wisdom and strength from adversity.

II. General Comments

A breakup is devastating to teens; they will be helped to use the pain for gain.

III. Possible Activities

a. Before session make photocopies of both the *From Ashes...* handouts, pages 121 and 122, and this Facilitator's page.
b. Cut this page on the broken line and retain the bottom (*From Fire...*) for Enrichment Activities.
c. If possible display a flower and a piece of golden jewelry.
d. Ask teens how these relate to romance (both may be gifts to signify love).
e. Ask how they are also linked to the pain of a breakup (answers will vary).
f. Distribute the *From Ashes...* handout; a volunteer reads the information in the box aloud.
g. Allow time for completion; encourage teens to share their responses.
h. Number 8 addresses a clean break using technology (block emails, no longer have the *ex* as a friend on social media, change cell phone number, block view of *ex's* activities on websites, etc.).
i. For number 9, teens write on the board some examples of negative and positive thoughts and receive feedback.
j. Ask teens how changing their thinking impacts their feelings and actions.

IV. Enrichment Activities

Continue the session, as homework or as a follow-up session.

a. Distribute the *From Fire...* handout below; a volunteer reads the quote aloud.
b. Allow time for completion; encourage teens to share their responses and receive peer feedback.

- -

From Fire ...

For gold must be tried by fire,
as a heart must be tried by pain!

~ Adelaide Anne Procter

My *flame* ______________________________

My pain ______________________________

My heart and I will emerge with these gold-like qualities:
Malleability – able to be shaped or bent without breaking.
Ductility – able to be stretched without breaking.
Resistance to corrosion – able to withstand weather without rusting.
Conductivity – able to transmit electric current.

I will shape myself into______________________________

I will stretch myself by ______________________________

I will survive storms by______________________________

I will transmit ______________________________

The refiner closely watches the gold in the furnace.

Who or what safeguards me? ______________________________

Too often we underestimate the power of a touch, a smile, a kind word, a listening ear, an honest compliment, or the smallest act of caring, all of which have the potential to turn a life around.

~ Leo Buscaglias

Diary of a Mensch

Mensch is a Yiddish and German word that means *"a person of integrity."*
A *mensch* is someone who is responsible, has a sense of right and wrong and is the sort of person other people look up to.

Fill in the blanks from this word bank.

agreed	**apologized**	**better**	**cry**	**depend**	**exhausted**	**grateful**	**helped**
know	**listened**	**picked**	**quiet**	**skipping**	**thanked**	**turned**	**tutor**

My Diary – Today

Last night I wanted to go out with friends. My parents/caregivers asked me to visit a sick relative. I ___________.

When I got home my friend who took the same biology class last year called me because he remembered some test questions. I ___________ him but said I'd rather not ___________.

I passed the test but the person who sits next to me failed. I offered to be a ___________.

On the way home I stopped at the store and almost slipped on a banana. I ___________ it up.

In the parking lot I saw two people kissing in a car. I know they were cheating on their partners. I was tempted to gossip about it but kept ___________.

At the gas station a customer was having trouble pumping gas. I ___________.

While I was walking to my car, I found a five dollar bill. I ___________ it in to the cashier.

When I arrived home my sister was hysterical because her partner broke up with her. I hugged her and let her ___________. Then I ___________ as she told me all about it.

By 6:00 p.m. I was ___________ and felt like ___________ work but I went because they ___________ on me.

Before bed I remembered I had argued with my friend during lunch. I called and ___________. I felt ___________ and know my friend did, too.

As I drifted off to sleep, I was ___________ for the day.

Diary of a Mensch

FOR THE FACILITATOR

I. Purpose

To identify positive attributes like integrity, responsibility, empathy, etc., that are common in a mensch.

II. General Comments

The diary entry will exemplify doing right and helping others with no expectation of something in return.

III. Possible Activities

a. If possible display a diary or journal and ask teens to share their experiences with confidential writing as well as their thoughts about the advantages and disadvantages.
b. Write *mensch* on the board and ask its meaning (a decent human being, a good person).
c. Distribute the *Diary of a Mensch* handout and review the directions.
d. Allow time for completion; encourage teens to share their responses.
The order of words for the blanks:

- agreed
- thanked
- know
- tutor
- picked
- quiet
- helped
- turned
- cry
- listened
- exhausted
- skipping
- depend
- apologized
- better
- grateful

e. Ask teens about times they exhibited these mensch-like traits:
1. Respect
2. Cooperation
3. Courage
4. Firmness of purpose

f. Encourage teens to share stories and memories about *mensches* they have known; remind them to use name codes or not use names at all.

IV. Enrichment Activities

Leo Rosten's definition of a mensch: *A mensch does the right thing the right way.*

Ask teens to brainstorm ways they can be *mensch-like* in the ways Mr. Rosten suggests below:

1. Help people who cannot help you.
2. Help without the expectation of return.
3. Pay back society.

Ask teens to brainstorm ways they can give back to society; a peer lists their ideas.

Possibilities:

- Donate money to charities.
- Volunteer at a human service agency.
- Help raise funds for a needy family.
- Work without pay for political, environmental or faith-based organizations.
- Perform random acts of kindness.
- Start up a charity.

Swapportunity

FUN LOVERS TEAM

Brainstorm activities you love to do in free time.

Examples
movies, video games, be with friends

1. ______________________
2. ______________________
3. ______________________
4. ______________________
5. ______________________
6. ______________________
7. ______________________
8. ______________________
9. ______________________
10. ______________________

FUNDRAISERS TEAM

Brainstorm causes to support with one fundraising idea for each.

Example: *A nephew with cancer; host a lemonade stand to raise money for medical expenses.*

1. Cause ______________________
   Fund Raiser ______________________
2. Cause ______________________
   Fund Raiser ______________________
3. Cause ______________________
   Fund Raiser ______________________
4. Cause ______________________
   Fund Raiser ______________________
5. Cause ______________________
   Fund Raiser ______________________
6. Cause ______________________
   Fund Raiser ______________________
7. Cause ______________________
   Fund Raiser ______________________
8. Cause ______________________
   Fund Raiser ______________________
9. Cause ______________________
   Fund Raiser ______________________
10. Cause ______________________
    Fund Raiser ______________________

Swapportunity

FOR THE FACILITATOR

I. Purpose

To encourage teens to support social causes (a cause is a principal, ideal, charity, goal or movement to which a person or group is dedicated) and view fundraisers as enjoyable and worthwhile pursuits.

II. General Comments

An opportunity to swap (*"swapportunity"*) self-activities for altruistic activities.

III. Possible Activities

a. Before session photocopy the *Swapportunity* handout; cut on the vertical line, one side per team.
b. Write *Free Time* on the board and ask what teens love to do in their free time (answers will vary).
c. Write *Causes to Support* on the board; ask teens to brainstorm while a peer lists their ideas.
   Example: Animals; spaying and neutering, aid to shelters, stopping puppy mills.
d. Write *Fundraisers* on the board and ask teens to brainstorm while a peer lists their ideas.
   Examples
   Car wash, bake sale, recycling projects; donate all proceeds to a charity.
e. Write *Swapportunity* on the board and explain teens will have the opportunity to swap one activity for another or to combine having fun and helping.
f. Divide teens into two teams – Give one team the *Fun Lovers* list and the other the *Fundraisers* list.
g. Team members huddle and a writer records their ideas.
h. Teams stand in two lines, facing each other, allowing enough room for a walkway between.
i. Teens from the *Fun Lovers* team will take turns walking down the path between the two teams.
j. At the start of the walk, each *Fun Lover* shares one beloved activity.
k. The *Fundraisers* team members decide on one of the causes and fundraisers to promote.
   Example: *Cause* – animals; *Fundraiser* – a car washing event.
l. With teens on each side, the *Fun Lover* walks down the path. Each teen in turn states a reason for the loved activity or taking part in the fundraiser.
   Examples
   - A *Fun Lover* shares a passion for video games as he/she starts the walk.
   - The first teen standing on the *Fun Lovers* side might say *"Think about your favorite games."*
   - The second teen on the *Fun Lovers* side might say *"You'll feel so great when you win."*
   - The first teen on the *Fundraisers* side might say *"Think of the starving shelter animals."*
   - The second teen on the *Fundraiser* side might say *"Think of the people you'll meet."*
m. When the *Fun Lover* reaches the end of the path and has heard all the arguments on each side, the teen decides whether to pursue the fun activity, help with the fundraiser, or combine a loved activity with a related cause and fundraiser.
   Example of combining
   - A photography buff might take pictures of shelter animals and show them at a car washing event; teens donate earnings to the shelter and the photographs promote animal adoptions.
n. The game continues as each *Fun Lover* shares a different preferred activity and the *Fundraisers* promote a different cause and fundraiser each round.
o. Each *Fun Lover* makes a decision for fun, fundraising or combining enjoyment and altruism.
p. It is best for teens to develop their own ideas;
   Some possibilities (if needed):
   Causes: Anti-Violence; Children; Disaster Relief; Education; Environment; Homelessness; Troops and Veterans; Physical and Mental Health Conditions; Addiction Recovery; Water-wells for the third world.

   Fund-Raisers: Charge admission for contests, games, concerts and performances by teens; create and sell booklets on any topic; create and sell a product; host a dance-a-thon or karaoke party; charge admission.

IV. Enrichment Activities

Encourage teens to adopt a group cause and facilitate a real-life fundraiser.

Care Contract

My Physical Health	My Mental Health	People At Home	My Extended Family
Example: *Exercise.* 1. How often? __________ 2. How often?	Example: *Write a song.* 1. How often? __________ 2. How often?	Example: *Ask about their day.* 1. How often? __________ 2. How often?	Example: *Visit relatives.* 1. How often? __________ 2. How often?

People At School	My Neighbors	My Community	My Country
Example: *Compliment people.* 1. How often? __________ 2. How often?	Example: *Take trash out for an elderly person.* 1. How often? __________ 2. How often?	Example: *Volunteer at a sporting event.* 1. How often? __________ 2. How often?	Example: *Correspond with the troops.* 1. How often? __________ 2. How often?

I promise myself to do the above activities to show that I care.

Signature ______________________________ Date ____________

Care Contract

FOR THE FACILITATOR

I. Purpose

To identify and implement ways to care about self and others.

II. General Comments

Teens broaden their spheres of influence starting with self and extending outward to their countries.

III. Possible Activities

a. Write *Care* on the board and ask what comes to mind (answers will vary).
b. Ask teens if they think it is selfish or sensible to care for their own health and why (sensible because they need to be in good condition to have the ability and energy to help others).
c. Distribute the *Care Contract* handout.
d. Allow time for completion.
e. Note that they need only two ideas under each heading.
f. Remind teens to decide how often they will perform each caring action (daily, weekly, etc.).
g. Encourage teens to sign the contract.
h. Explain that teens will share their responses.
i. Volunteers take turns writing one of the headings from their paper on the board.
j. Volunteers elicit at least five ideas for each heading.
k. Each volunteer or a different teen lists the group's ideas on the board.

Possibilities

My Physical Health	My Mental Health	People At Home	My Extended Family
Eat healthy foods, get adequate sleep, wear sunscreen, avoid alcohol, nicotine and illegal drugs, prevent unwanted pregnancy and STDs.	Share issues with a trusted adult, express feelings via art, music, poetry, etc., find a balance between work and play, be assertive, use positive self-talk.	Clean-up after myself, help with household chores, compromise, communicate, share TV, computer, phone, etc., respect parents and/or caregivers, comply with rules.	Help elderly relatives with yard work, technology or chores, help younger relatives with schoolwork or sports, send or give cards or notes for birthdays, etc.
People At School	**My Neighbors**	**My Community**	**My Country**
Become a peer tutor or mentor, anonymously report bullies, befriend people who are different, include shy people in conversations, tell staff if a peer wants to harm self or others.	Visit people who are lonely, help people unload groceries, go to the pharmacy for a sick person, tutor children, put the newspaper near a disabled person's door.	Keep dogs on leashes and clean-up after them, don't litter, volunteer at homeless shelters, organize a fund-raiser for a local cause, join a community theater or other cultural activities.	Preserve the environment by using paper bags rather than plastic, recycle, work for environmental, political, and social causes, promote research and funds for disease cures.

IV. Enrichment Activities

Encourage teens to save their contracts and revisit the issues weekly. Discuss ways that teens do not always follow through and how they can better uphold their commitments. Discuss rewards of caring.

What's My Cause?

MYSTERY GUEST – You are the **AIDS Research Alliance**

You may answer only *Yes* or *No* to contestant questions.

FYI:

AIDS is a disease of the immune system caused by infection with the HIV retrovirus.

You can find ways to prevent the disease.

If contestants have not guessed your identity after 5 questions give the following clues (one at a time):

- Spread through blood and body fluids.
- Victims can't fight infections.

MYSTERY GUEST – You are **PetSmart Charities**

You may answer only *Yes* or *No* to contestant questions.

FYI:

You promote adoptions of homeless pets and help stop needless animal euthanasia.

You help with emergency relief for animals suffering from disasters.

You are affiliated with the stores that sell pet supplies and services.

If contestants have not guessed your identity after 5 questions give the following clues (one at a time):

- Animal adoptions at stores.
- Title means that domesticated animals are brilliant.

MYSTERY GUEST – You are the **Christopher and Dana Reeve Foundation**

You may answer only *Yes* or *No* to contestant questions.

FYI:

You help fund research to find a cure for spinal cord injuries.

You help improve the quality of life for people who are paralyzed.

If contestants have not guessed your identity after 5 questions give the following clues (one at a time):

- Severely injured actor.
- Superman.

MYSTERY GUEST – You are **Habitat for Humanity**

You may answer only *Yes* or *No* to contestant questions.

FYI:

You build and repair houses internationally using donations and volunteer laborers.

You help people who are homeless, living in slums or who lost homes due to disasters.

If contestants have not guessed your identity after 5 questions give the following clues (one at a time):

- Everyone needs a safe and decent place to live.
- Teens and adults alike help build.

What's My Cause?

FOR THE FACILITATOR

I. Purpose

To consider a variety of causes and develop an interest in social issues.

II. General Comments

Teens portray and guess the identity of personified causes and participate in advocacy activities.

III. Possible Activities

a. Ask for the defiinition of a "cause" *(a cause is a principal, ideal, charity, goal or movement to which a person or group is dedicated).*
b. Before session photocopy the two *What's My Cause?* handouts pages 131 and 133.
c. Cut on the broken lines and place cutouts face down in the front of the room.
d. Explain that teens will portray Mystery Guest causes, described on the cutouts.
e. Volunteers take turns picking up a cutout, silently reading the description.
f. The audience contestants take turns asking questions of the person who read the cutout. Questions can be answered with *Yes* or *No* only.
g. If teens have difficulty developing questions, review some possibilities.
Possibilities
- Do you help people?
- Do you help animals?
- Do you mostly help adults?
- Do you mostly help children?
- Is your main focus a disease?
- Do you mostly help people living in poverty?
- Do you focus on people with disabilities?
- Do you help people who have been injured?
- Do you have an educational emphasis?
- Do you provide employment and training?

h. The above list is repeated on page 134 to photocopy and distribute to teens, as an alternate to formulating questions.
i. If contestants haven't guessed the cause's identity after five questions they ask for a clue.
j. Two clues are provided for each; the teen who guesses correctly plays the next Mystery Guest.
k. If no one guesses after five questions and two clues, the Mystery Guest reveals the cause.
l. Mystery Guests may read aloud their causes' descriptions before the next Mystery Guest starts.
m. After all the cut-outs are played, encourage teens to think about other worthwhile causes.
n. Volunteers may play Mystery Guests regarding a cause they have in mind.
o. Mystery Guests answer up to five *Yes* or *No* questions and provide two clues as in the game described above.

IV. Enrichment Activities

a. Photocopy the *Advocacy in Action* handout on page 134.
b. Distribute the bottom of the page to all teens.
c. Encourage teens individually or in teams to select an advocacy method and create an advertisement.
d. Teens may promote one of the causes used in the game or one they are passionate about.
e. Encourage teens to share their work and/or perform their mock videos or other productions.

(Enrichment Activities continued on page 134)

What's My Cause? *(Continued)*

MYSTERY GUEST – You are the **Special Olympics**

You may answer only *Yes* or *No* to contestant questions.

FYI:

Through sports you transform the lives of people with disabilities.

You help them develop skills and confidence through training and competitions.

If contestants have not guessed your identity after 5 questions give the following clues (one at a time):

- Through the power of sports, world games celebrate differences.
- Started by Eunice Kennedy Shriver.

MYSTERY GUEST – You are **Big Brothers/Big Sisters of America**

You may answer only *Yes* or *No* to contestant questions.

FYI:

You pair children with role models or mentors.

Children involved with you are less likely to use alcohol or drugs or to skip school.

If contestants have not guessed your identity after 5 questions give the following clues (one at a time):

- Kids need someone to look up to.
- Means Older Sibling.

MYSTERY GUEST – You are **Scholarship America**

You may answer only *Yes* or *No* to contestant questions.

FYI:

You help fund education after high school and provide tuition assistance.

You help students stay in school when they are faced with unforeseen financial emergencies.

If contestants have not guessed your identity after 5 questions give the following clues (one at a time):

- Good grades help.
- Financial Aid.

MYSTERY GUEST – You are **Goodwill Industries International, Inc.**

You may answer only *Yes* or *No* to contestant questions.

FYI:

You provide training and employment for people who have disabilities or disadvantages.

You help people reach their full potential and lead productive lives.

If contestants have not guessed your identity after 5 questions give the following clues (one at a time):

- Donations.
- Thrift Stores.

MYSTERY GUEST – You are **4H**

You may answer only *Yes* or *No* to contestant questions.

FYI:

You provide youth development programs with a focus on leadership, citizenship and life skills.

You started with an agricultural emphasis but serve youth in all types of communities today.

If contestants have not guessed your identity after 5 questions give the following clues (one at a time):

- Head, Heart, Hands and Health.
- Earn prizes at county fairs.

What's My Cause?

FOR THE FACILITATOR *(continued from 132)*

IV. Enrichment Activities *(continued from page 132)*

a. You may photocopy this page and cut out the top ten boxes on the broken lines.
b. These are an alternate to teens formulating their own questions.
c. Teens may pick up one of the cutouts and ask the question when it is their turn.

Possible contestant questions to ask mystery guests

Do you help people?	Do you help animals?	Do you mostly help adults?	Do you mostly help children?	Is your main focus a disease?
Do you mostly help people living in poverty?	Do you focus on people with disabilities?	Do you help people who have been injured?	Do you have an educational emphasis?	Do you provide employment and training?

For ***Advocacy in Action***

a. Photocopy enough copies of this page for all participants and cut on the broken line below.
b. Distribute the *Advocacy in Action* section of this handout below.
c. Encourage teens individually or in teams to select an advocacy method and create an advertisement.
d. Teens may promote one of the causes used in the *What's My Cause?* game or any issue they are passionate about.
e. Encourage teens to share their work and/or perform their mock videos or other productions.

Advocacy in Action

Select one of the methods below or dream up your own.
Promote one of the causes used in the *What's My Cause?* game or an issue you are passionate about.

1. Make a mock video promoting your cause.
2. Select a few *panelists* and, as the moderator, interview them about their causes.
3. Compose (on paper) an email message to recruit people for your cause.
4. Create (on paper) an online web homepage with a catchy name to interest people in your cause.
5. Write a few brief imaginary testimonials from people or animals helped by your cause.
6. Create a poster promoting your cause.
7. Compose a radio or TV infomercial about your cause.
8. Write a song and/or lyrics about your cause.
9. Write a poem or jingle (catchy tune or verse) to advertise your cause.
10. Use your imagination and develop your own advocacy approach.

Leadership: Passion or Power?

Leadership is the ability to guide and influence people; to organize a group to achieve a common goal.

Passion is intense enthusiasm for a subject or activity.

However, leadership that seeks **power** for its own sake is destructive.

The most powerful weapon on earth is the human soul on fire. ~ Field Marshall Ferdinand Foch

Compassion ignited these leaders:

- A young person saw a man eat out of a dumpster and raised funds for homeless people.
- A young person read about a boy murdered in a foreign country for speaking out against child labor and started an organization to raise awareness about exploitation.
- A young person realized that kids from troubled homes often leave with only the clothes on their backs and started a care bag charity to provide shampoo, toothbrushes, soap, toys, etc.
- A teenage artist started an organization to give art supplies to impoverished kids in Latin America.
- A young person whose sibling was born with a serious sickness made and sold bracelets to help diminish childhood diseases.

Pretend you are the president of a new service club.
If your members have a burning desire to meet a need, fan the flame!
If they need ideas, check out these possibilities:

- Start a fund for peers who need food, clothes, school supplies, money for extracurricular activities.
- Mentor students who need tutoring.
- Fundraise to obtain new technology or sports equipment needed at school.
- Advocate for programs that were cut from the budget.
- Campaign to start new programs or subjects that are needed at school.
- Take action to stop bullying.
- *Turn on* students who have *tuned out* education.
- Set up a program to improve attendance and timeliness.
- Write letters to military members who are friends or relatives of students.

1. Lead your team to describe who you will help or what you will improve. ______________________

   ____

2. Lead your team to describe how you will accomplish your goal(s). ______________________

   ____

3. Lead your team to name your club. ______________________________________

   ____

4. Lead your team to imagine three advertising ideas.
   1) ____
   2) ____
   3) ____

5. Lead your team to plan three fundraising events.
   1) ____
   2) ____
   3) ____

Leadership: Passion or Power?

FOR THE FACILITATOR

I. Purpose

To develop leadership skills in the context of starting a possible service club.

II. General Comments

Teens are encouraged to inspire and help others rather than pursue power for self-serving purposes.

III. Possible Activities

a. Write *Leadership* on the board; teens brainstorm traits of a good leader; a peer lists ideas on board.

- Ability to delegate
- Assertive
- Committed
- Communicator
- Compassionate
- Creative
- Credits others
- Dedicated
- Fair
- Forward-looking
- Honest
- Humble
- Confident and able to inspire confidence
- Inspirational
- Intuitive
- Open to new ideas
- Positive attitude
- Sense of humor

b. Ask teens to identify leadership roles they have or will have in the future (mentors for younger siblings or relatives, school or work project leaders, youth group leaders, lifeguards, tutors, band leaders, sports and recreation leaders, camp counselors, peer counselors, etc.)

c. Ask teens to describe people in leadership roles who misuse power (adults who abuse children, bosses who degrade employees, political leaders who oppress citizens, etc.).

d. Ask teens to brainstorm ways they could provide hands-on help or raise funds for improvement. Possibilities are noted on the handout.

e. Distribute the *Leadership: Passion or Power?* handout; volunteers read aloud up to the numbered items.

f. Depending on the number of teens in group, ask for enough volunteer leaders so that each leader has three or more team members.

g. Allow leaders and team members to sit together; leaders or volunteers document responses on the handout.

h. The group re-convenes and leaders share their teams' ideas and receive feedback.

i. Ask team members to share how their leaders inspired them to develop a dream.

j. Repeat this session periodically until all teens have the chance to be leaders.

IV. Enrichment Activities

a. Ask teens to discuss and debate whether leaders are born or made.

b. Encourage teens to actually start a service club or awareness campaign. Possibilities include school-related improvements on the handout plus helping people or improving conditions involving science, education, human rights, cruelty prevention, physical or mental health, safety, sports, the arts, etc.

Whole Person Associates is the leading publisher of training resources for professionals who empower people to create and maintain healthy lifestyles. Our creative resources will help you work effectively with your clients in the areas of stress management, wellness promotion, mental health and life skills.

Please visit us at our web site: **www.wholeperson.com**. You can check out our entire line of products, place an order, request our print catalog, and sign up for our monthly special notifications.

Whole Person Associates

800-247-6789